Virginie Barré
Ernesto Caivano
Lotte Konow Lund
Mindaugas Lukosaitis
Barry McGee
Julie Mehretu
Paul Noble
Wilhelm Sasnal
Morten Schelde
Inga Svala Thorsdottir

ON LINE

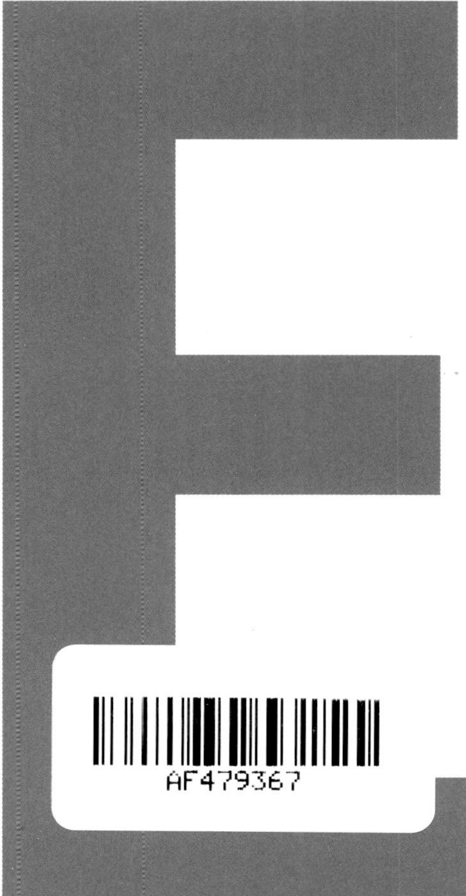

Preface

For close to a decade now there has been an overwhelming interest in drawing among the artists of the day, as evidenced by among other events MoMa's major *Drawing Now* exhibition in 2002 and most recently by the book *Vitamin D* from Phaidon Press, which is appearing concurrently with Louisiana's exhibition. So the time is clearly ripe for Louisiana to present, in the context of the LOUISIANA CONTEMPORARY series, a selection of artists who have used drawing strikingly as a form of expression and to examine what the medium has to offer in the overall field of the visual arts right now.

The title of the exhibition points to two factors. One is that the basic drawing function, the *line*, is still central to the idiom; the other is that drawing still involves the relationship between the artist's body and the surface of the paper, on which any correction is visible to the eye of the beholder. The digital community, on the other hand, which puts everything and everyone on-line, is still to some extent alien to drawing, an antithesis that plays a role – for this is *on line*, not on-line. However, if drawing has remained revelatory, reflective and slow, on the other hand it has come to fruition as never before as a medium in its own right. In contemporary art it is an independent field of work among others – not only the genre of practice, preparation and sketch.

Many people have been helpful to the museum in connection with the organization and implementation of the exhibition. Our thanks first to the artists: Virginie Barré, Ernesto Caivano, Lotte Konow Lund, Mindaugas Lukosaitis, Barry McGee, Julie Mehretu, Paul Noble, Wilhelm Sasnal, Morten Schelde and Inga Svala Thorsdottir; then to the gallery-owners and lenders for their willing help. Thanks to Hervé Loevenbruck, Galerie Loevenbruck Paris, Ulrich Gebauer, carlier | gebauer, Berlin, Nina Paus, Galleri Wang, Oslo; Vita Zaman Cookson, IBID PROJECTS, London & Vilnius, Contemporary Art Centre CAC Vilnius, Stuart Shave | Modern Art, London, Paula Feldman and Jay Jopling, White Cube, London, Maureen Paley, Maureen Paley, London, Sadie Coles, Sadie Coles HQ, London and Susanne Ottesen and Gustav Gimm, Galleri Susanne Ottesen, Copenhagen. And thanks to Sammlung Falckenberg, Hamburg and private lenders who have wished to remain anonymous.

Finally, my gratitude to the curators of the exhibition, Anders Kold and Mette Marcus, and to the curatorial coordinator Marianne Ahrensberg. As always, the museum is grateful to its sponsors for the support they give to the activities of the museum – so our heartfelt thanks to Nykredit, which is sponsoring Louisiana Contemporary. Thanks too to Realdania Foundation – the sponsor of Louisiana's architectural exhibitions – and to DONG, the principal sponsor of Louisiana's exhibitions.

Poul Erik Tøjner
Director, Louisiana Museum of Modern Art

This catalogue has been published on the occasion of the exhibition
LOUISIANA CONTEMPORARY: ON LINE
November 5, 2005 – January 22, 2006
Curators: Anders Kold and Mette Marcus
Coordinator: Marianne Ahrensberg
Introductory texts by Anders Kold
Catalogue edited by Michael Juul Holm and Anders Kold
© Louisiana Museum of Modern Art and the contributors
All works © the artists, reproduction material courtesy
Virginie Barré: Galerie Hervé Loevenbruck, Paris
Ernesto Caivano: carlier | gebauer, Berlin
(Photo: Stefan Maria Rother, Berlin)
Lotte Konow Lund: Galleri Wang, Oslo
Mindaugas Lukosaitis: Ibid Projects, London & Vilnius
Barry McGee: Stuart Shave | Modern Art,
London (Photo: Andy Keate)
Julie Mehretu: Private Collection, Courtesy White Cube,
London (Photo: Stephen White)
Paul Noble: Maureen Paley, London
Wilhelm Sasnal: Sadie Coles HQ, London
Graphic design by Steen Heide
Translations from the Danish by James Manley
Printed by Rosendahls Bogtrykkeri, Esbjerg
ISBN: 87-91607-18-3
Printed in Denmark 2005

Nykredit Sponsor of LOUISIANA CONTEMPORARY

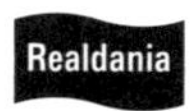 The Foundation Realdania.
Sponsor of architectural exhibitions at Louisiana

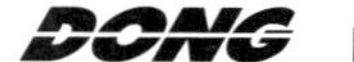 Main sponsor of exhibitions at Louisiana

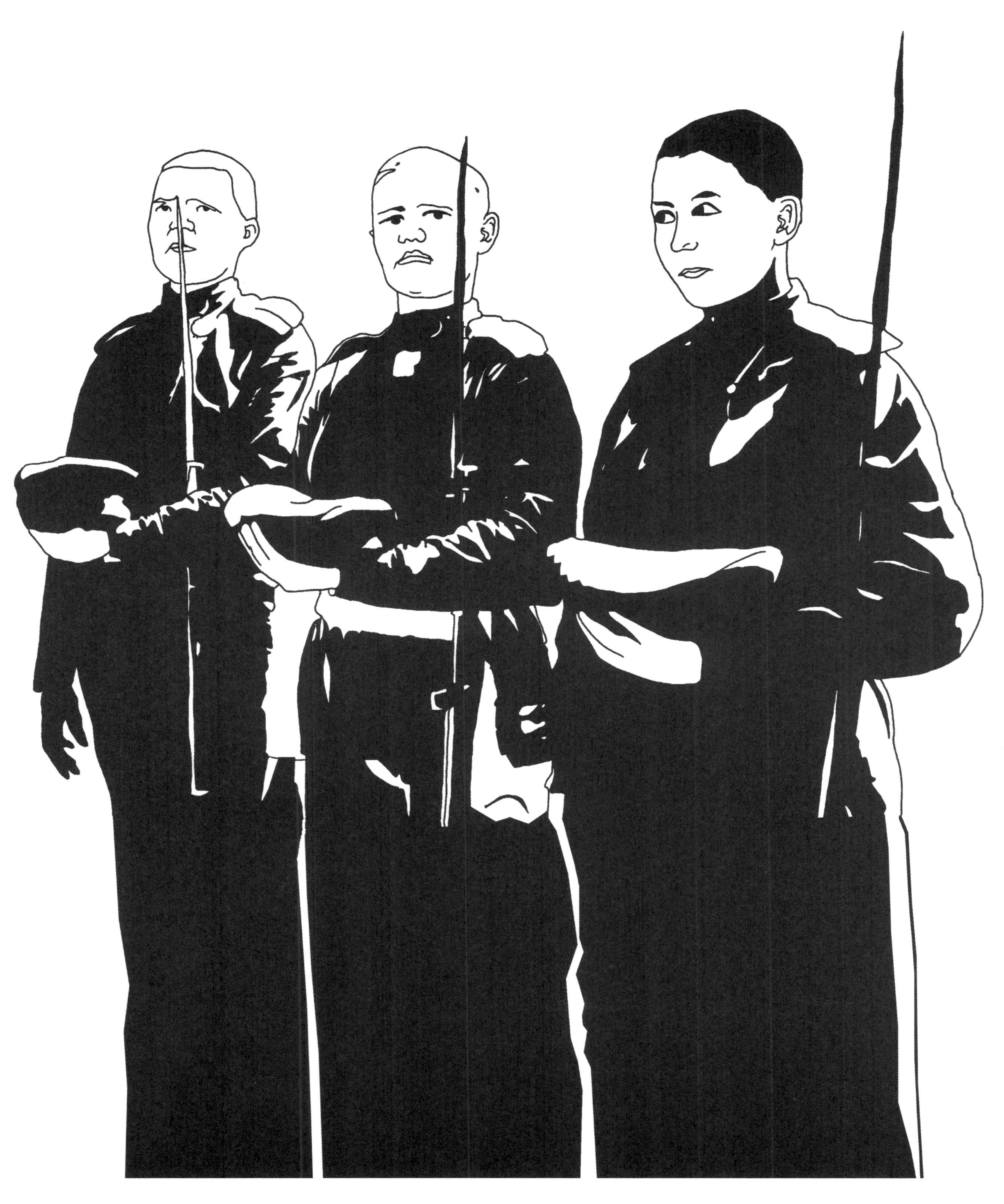

Historical figures – and all of them women. Some of them genuinely historical figures, people who have gone down in history as recognizable individuals in public circulation; others anonymous, but historical in another sense, as human décor and links with the historical events of an epoch. There is nothing intrinsically new about emphasizing the share of women in forging the chains of history, but here we have not just one type of women – the suffragettes or the battle-ready daughters of the Russian Revolution, that sort of thing – but also for example the first generation of women to wear real bathing costumes, and the anonymous figures of the war years in their elegant *ersatz* clothes. And then we must note that the work *Women* does not develop in a linear motion through time – so as a classic political project it fails on all counts. But it is political in its own way, and at all events it is drawing in a different way, since the 36 sheets were created on a computer and later printed out on something that looks like photographic paper. The doors to the chambers of film and photography stand wide open.

You soon realize that this is not about pinning as many unique, exotic species as possible to the wall like some butterfly collector. Feminism, if that is what is at play in Barré's work, makes its impact in a different way – in the investigation of and confrontation with stereotypes and clichés as a whole. The choice of medium – we even have an edition here – could hardly be further removed from the fêted one-offs of classic hand-drawing. The cliché is isolated, it stands there remote and constructed, as in many other works where Barré's practice has been to encode the emotional registers of the B and horror movie as everyday scenarios, furnishing them with potential for other contexts. Thus both classic horror films like *The Shining* and space operas have been filtered through everyday space, with an impactful mixture of youthful apathy, adult slacking a-go-go and Superman in the suburbs as the result; typically in installation form, and often, in that context, with drawing in the role of an interface between different media and idioms; in other words as the locus of linguistic exchange. Here the fields of fiction intersect, scenes become remakes, periods are spliced together and surprising encounters are produced. What we see here is the drawing as a conceptual tool rather than as a medium with a variety of formal registers to play on.

Technically, with its computer graphics technique, *Women* steps out of the nostalgic tonalities of film and photography; in a certain sense the air is siphoned off from the idiom. And so drawing can become cold turkey, just as the *flip book* genre that Barré has used in several contexts can gear the film medium down to 'slow'. In this light the 36 heroines have been constructed anew, extracted and reinstalled in something that is at all events not just some pocket of resistance in relation to the fluctuations of the contemporary.

Virginie Barré
Born 1970. Lives and works in Nantes and Douarnenez, France

Selected Solo Exhibitions

2005
Simple Dames, Galerie Loevenbruck, Paris, France
El corte françes, ADN Galerià, Barcelona, Spain

2004
Ecarlate, FRAC Basse-Normandie, Caen, France
Starting Game, Musée des Beaux-Arts de Bordeaux, France
Les gras, École des Beaux-Arts, Galerie Edouard Manet, Gennevilliers, France

2003
Overlook, Le Parvis, Pau, France

2002
Virginie Barré, Palais de Tokyo, Paris, France

2001
Galerie Loevenbruck, Paris, France
Drawing Quake, Parker's Box Gallery, NY, USA

2000
Journey to the Center of the Universe, Tramway, Glasgow, UK
Parallel Universe, Independent Project Room, Glasgow, UK

Selected Group Exhibitions

2005
8th Biennale de Lyon 2005, Lyon, France
Offshore, Espace Paul Ricard, Paris, France
WA, Surface d'autonomie temporaire, Palais de Tokyo, Paris, France
Draw!, Galerie du jour Agnès B, Paris, France
I still believe in miracles, Musée d'Art Moderne de la Ville de Paris, France
The Morning After the Night Before, Parker's Box Gallery, Brooklyn, New York, USA

2004
Parker's Box Gallery, NY, USA
Diesel Gallery & Surface 2 air, New York, USA
ADN Galerie, Barcelona, Spain
Museum of York, Pennsylvania, USA

2003
Action-Man-Oeuvres #4, Carbaret Alétoire, Marseille, France
Oxymory, FRAC Basse Normandie, Caen, France
Extra, Swiss Institute, New York, USA
Walde - Ganne - Maquet - Barré, Villa Arson, Nice, Nizza, France

2002
Ouverture, Palais de Tokyo, Paris
Art at the turn of the rue de Seine et la rue de l'Echaudée, Galerie Loevenbruck, Paris, France
French Touch days, Club La Fabrique, Tokyo, Japan
La Force de l'Esprit, Espace Pierre Cardin, Paris, France
Récits, Abbaye Saint-André, Centre d'Art Contemporain, Meymac, France

2001
Computer Cosmos, Galerie Francoise Vigna, Nice, France

2000
Parallel Universe, Independant Project Room, Glasgow, UK

1999
Spazierengehen, Künstlerhaus Bethanien, Hamburg, Germany

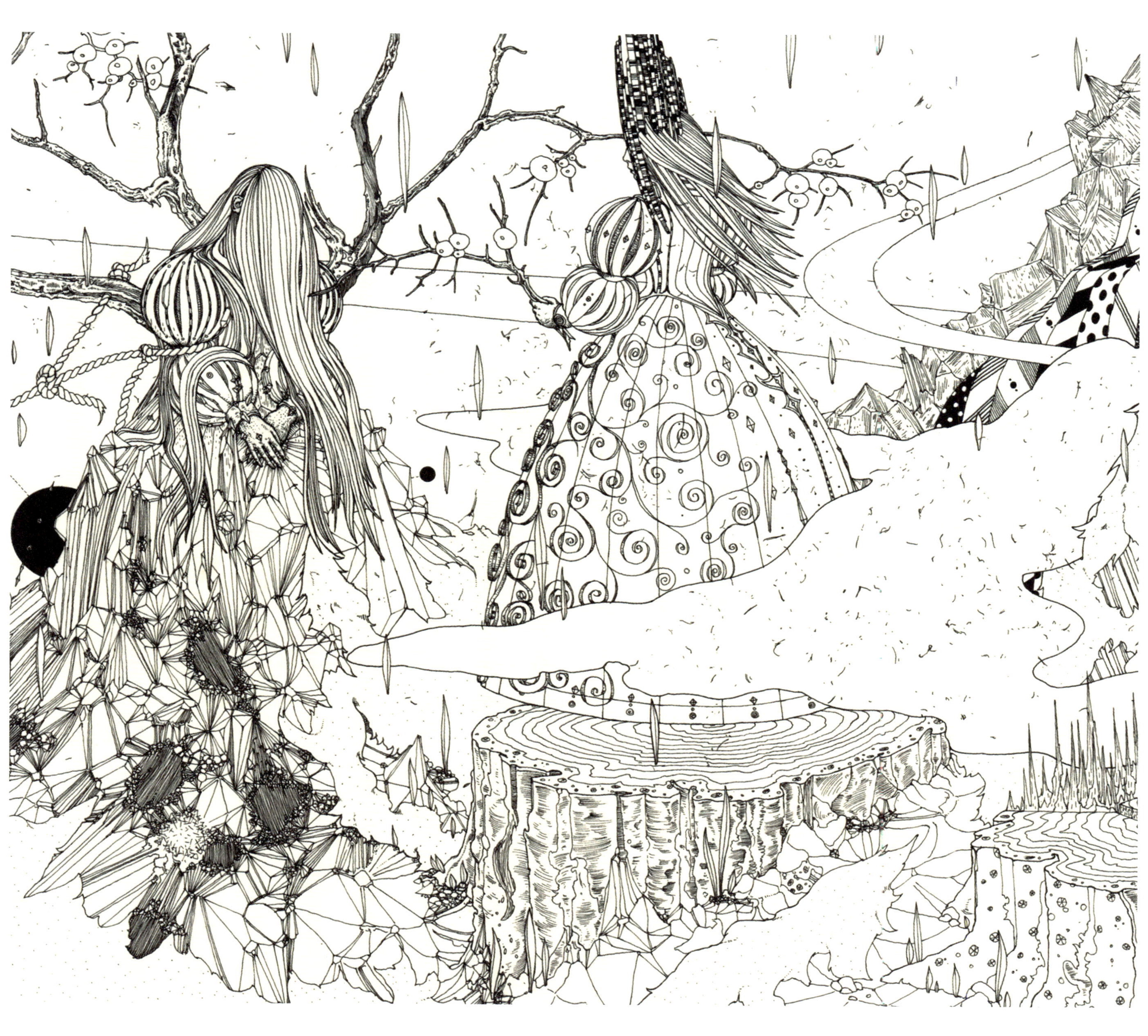

Ernesto Caivano

One of the themes that has been emphasized as characteristic of drawing today is a kind of romantic Utopianism. And at first glance it is tempting to include Caivano in this camp; but on closer examination and reflection it becomes less clear whether this is in fact so – even though the tendency of the artworks is to relate rather literally to a universe somewhere between medieval Holy-Grailery and Baroquerie in a more contemporary sense. But out of the superabundance of the archetypal narrative – tailored to a man/knight and woman/queen pattern – new structures are constantly crystallizing. It is possible that the story as such develops, but in its morphology and linguistic structure this whole perspective undergoes a transformation in a more conceptual direction. For example, with Caivano's extremely meticulous, almost ornamental use of the line, one can note with a certain sense of liberation that drawing today is not only practiced by women, sculpting their contours like fine needlework, while the men only draw (the) broad lines. In the handed-down relations between the genders too drawing is well on its way to transcending its own and the world's conventions.

On careful scrutiny of Caivano's drawings – right down to the character of the line and the significance it is given – one will see how the narrative structure is dissolved in a process where everything is constantly flowing in and over everything else. No principle is fundamentally female and no spear-headed crystal remains male. It is a kind of infinity that unfolds, where the reading of the signs from detail to panoramic horizon renounces singularity of meaning. By definition, detail captures something to do with precision, and panorama creates overview; but here neither is presented with any certainty. So is there any meaning and congruence at all behind these Lewis Carroll-like shifts between reality and fiction? The viewer must necessarily forgo the overview in Caivano's drawing-installations and surrender to the moment and the subjective perspective; the cognitive potential of the works lies precisely in the flow of information with which we are presented, and which we process in our own reading. And with the exhibited work what we are offered, with extraordinary physical presence, is a kind of performative appropriation. The leaps and the relative loss of control that arise along the way are the consistency of the work. So what we see is in a certain sense a kind of networks in *drag*, models for ongoing projections on the white surface of the paper. And not unlike Kandinsky's apocalyptic horsemen almost a century ago, it is the transformation of the very fabric of the world that is taking place.

Ernesto Caivano
Born 1972, Madrid, Spain. Lives and works in New York, USA

Education

2001
MFA Columbia University
1999
BFA The Cooper Union

Selected Solo Exhibitions

2005
Ernesto Caivano, Sutton Lane, London, UK
Union and Offerings, carlier | gebauer, Berlin, Germany

2004
After the Woods: A Selection – P.S.1 Contemporary Art Center, New York, NY, USA
Mating Grounds, Richard Heller Gallery, Los Angeles, CA, USA
In the Woods, Long-term installation at P.S.1 Contemporary Art Center, New York, NY, USA

2003
Arboreal - 31 Grand Inc., Brooklyn, NY, USA

Selected Group Exhibitions

2005
Hallucinations, Galerie Almine Rech, Paris, France
Sutton Lane in Paris, Galerie Ghislaine Hussenot, Paris, France
Greater New York 2005, P.S.1 Contemporary Art Center, New York, NY, USA
Can't See the Forest, Sixspace, Los Angeles, CA, USA

2004
Instinctive, Andrea Rosen Gallery, New York, NY, USA
I Feel Mysterious Today, Palm Beach Institute of Contemporary Art, FL, USA
Pick-up Lines, Geoffrey Young Gallery, Great Barrington, MA, USA
Happy Days Are Here Again, David Zwirner, New York, NY, USA
Woodwork, Anthony Grant, Inc., New York, NY, USA
How Would You Light Heaven, carlier | gebauer, Berlin, Germany
Whitney Biennial 2004, Whitney Museum of American Art, New York, NY, USA

2003
My Sources Says Yes, Guild & Greyshkul, New York, NY, USA
Terrarium, Bronx River Art Center, Bronx, NY, USA
Druid Wood as a Superconductor, Space 101, Brooklyn, NY, USA
The New Topography, Geoffrey Young Gallery, Great Barrington, MA, USA
Group Show, Grant / Selwyn Fine Art, LA, USA
St. Valentine's Day Massacre, 85 Chambers, New York, NY, USA

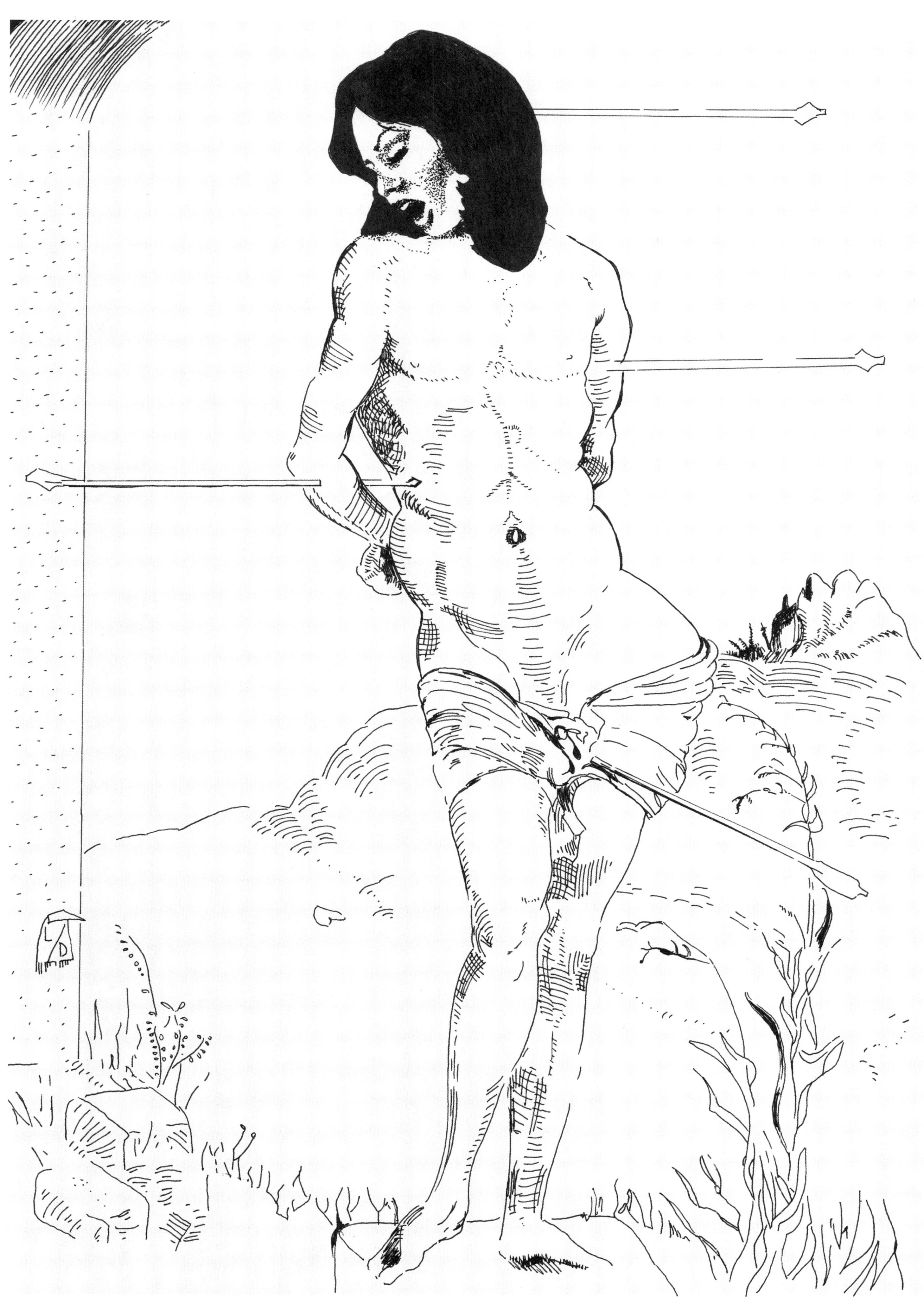

Lotte Konow Lund

The concept of "borrowed plumes" need not be understood as a negative characteristic of an artist's activity today; in fact it is coming to be seen as a condition of art; especially because the formal distinctions, stylistic ones for example, are being given less weight than the intentional or discursive thrust of the artwork. So when Lotte Konow Lund, in the 29-sheet series *Let It Go – the Dürer Drawings*, with its specific model in the German Renaissance master, adds angels' wings to her thinly contoured up-to-the minute lines, this is a deliberate, pointedly gross clash of aesthetics. No important artists draw today like Albrecht Dürer – they simply can't – but the point is anyway elsewhere; as for example in Cindy Sherman's work, one deciphers the *mise-en-scène* of the tableau rather than attempting to grasp it with the eyes of a taxidermist.

The art-historical models in the 29 sheets should be compared to stage sets, to scenery in a work which with its extent and a basic narrative structure that approaches the loop, points towards performance art – and not least towards Lotte Konow Lund's own video productions. Directed role-playing with accompanying props, which in principle consist of Dürer's *The Martyrdom of St. Sebastian* from 1499, but which are transformed along the way with loans from the film diva Marilyn Monroe, a feminist saint like Lynda Benglis and the high priest of ambiguity Marcel Duchamp in the role of Rose Sélavy. The last of these in itself a *mise-en-scène* and an iconic work as regards both the frailty of the vessel and the authorial subject.

And after all, this whole postmodern theatre could probably have been played out in other media, but the clashes and the chimeric constructions – the whole fictionalization of the baggage from the great tradition – are manifested with great clarity in the drawing on the paper. Dislocated hips, dislocated history, dislocated gender, the dislocated status of the viewer – and thus in a certain sense also dislocated drawing. An assault of the now, in a medium of the now, on the whole western iconology that we have been able to look up since 1593 in the Italian Cesare Ripa's *Iconologia*. A catalogue of the conceptual coordinates of the western world, inspiration with strings attached. Or as Konow Lund in 1997 called a video, *I Know 100 Ways to Be a Good Girl*.

Lotte Konow Lund
Born 1967, Oslo. Lives and works in Oslo, Norway

Education

1993-97
The National Academy of Fine Arts, Oslo
1992-93
The Art School in Rogaland

Selected solo exhibitions

2005
Galleri Wang, Oslo, Norway

2002
IASKA, International Art Space Kellerberrin, Australia

2001
Solitude For Many, Galleri Wang, Oslo, Norway
Wohnmachine, Berlin, Germany

2000
Yet another victory that makes me smaller, Galleri Brandstrup, Stavanger, Norway

1999
Video Works 98/99, Galleri Wang, Oslo, Norway

1997
I know 100 ways to be a good girl, Gallery G.I., Nationaltheater, Oslo, Norway

Selected group exhibitions

2005
Munch Revisited – Edvard Munch und die heutige Kunst, Museum am Ostwall, Dortmund, Germany

2004
VIDEO ZONE - The 2nd International Video- Art Biennial in Israel, Tel Aviv, Israel

2003
Rest in Space/Berlin, The Künstlerhouse Bethanien, Berlin, Germany
Cinema Paradiso, Galleri Charlotte Lund, Stockholm, Sweden

2002
Collectors Item, Galleri F-15, Moss
Contemporary Art and Video, Moderna Museet, Stockholm, Sweden; Istanbul Museum of Modern Art, Turkey; Borås Konstmuseum, Sweden, Norrköpings Art Museum, Sweden, Kunstnernes Hus, Oslo, Norway
Extreme Existence, Pratt Manhattan Gallery, New York, USA
Norwegian Slacker Drawing, Drammen Art Museum, Norway

2001
Kunst und Kur. Ästethik der Arholung, Kunsthaus Meran, Meran, Italy
Blick Festival, Touring exhibition, org. by Nifca
Error one, Art and Media Centre, Berlin Adlershof, Germany

2000
Cross Female, Künstlerhaus Bethanien, Berlin, Germany
eMotion Picture, Galleri F-15, Moss, Norway
Oslo Open, Henie Onstad Kunstersenter, Oslo, Norway

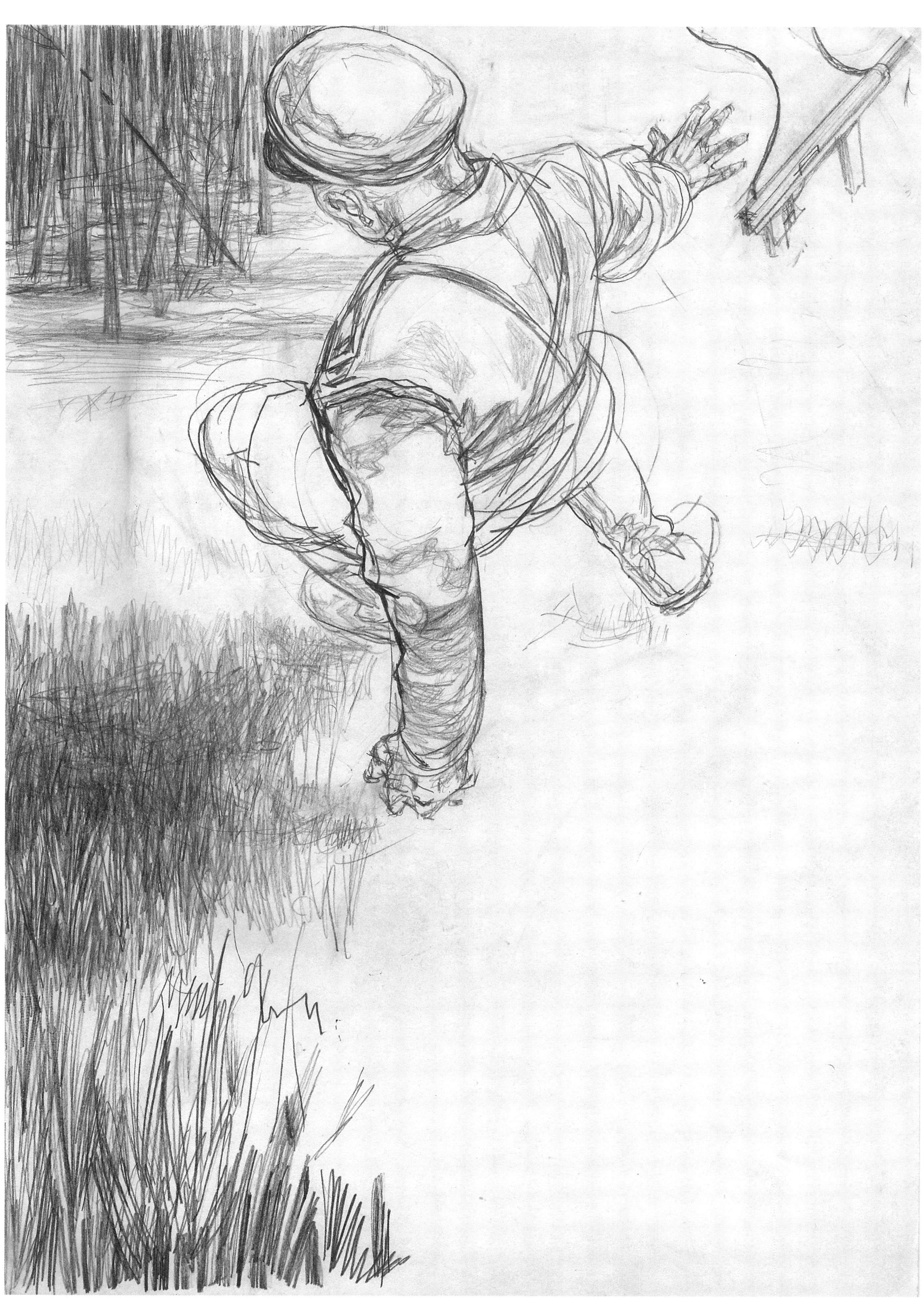

Mindaugas Lukosaitis

The theme, or at least the motivic starting-point for Mindaugas Lukosaitis' long series of drawings, is the Lithuanian partisan war against the occupying Russian forces from the end of World War II all the way down to the mid-fifties. But the foreignness of the project, the very distance from the events, is at the same time an issue and probably the true artistic mainspring. And the distance is also the condition of grasping the subject at all. For as long as the artist has been able to reflect over his national heritage the country has in fact been an independent state, and now also a liberal democracy within the European Union.

Making pictures of something remote in time, a time which for the artist cannot even be said to live in memory, is difficult. Doing so, as is the case, without documentary or other material that can give the project authenticity, seems impossible. So what points of reference – and what intentions – does the fiction have? The imaginative potential of drawing undoubtedly lies behind the actual choice of medium. One could imagine the same material treated with the resources of video, for example the documentation of older compatriots with roots back in this traumatic period in the history of the country. One can easily envisage it. But here the formal training of the artist – Lukosaitis can really draw – overlaps with a more or less formulated wish for loyalty to the mythological, indeed the whole popular and national spirit of the project; which thus argues in favour of describing this as a kind of conceptual folk art.

The whole project is reflected on the epic scale, but is faithful to its own (small) scale too by not pointing to any precise narrative order. Nevertheless it is a highly unusual work with both exotic and particularly relevant points of access for the contemporary viewer – in the fundamental clash between *verismo* and total fiction, but also in the diversity of dramatic resources used. The absence of actual documentary material activates images from the collective memorial archives: arrays of fighting and falling figures are available as a matrix in most people's consciousness; and here Lukosaitis is clearly working with devices from both the comic strip and the photographic and filmic media. But there are other places in the series where (if it were not for the fateful mode of the subject) the landscape evocations lie closest to the gaze of the ornithological illustrator; a true rarity in the contemporary art world, but not so strange given the concrete circumstances of the artist's life: he lives in the forest. The *mix*, on the other hand, the subtle and sometimes almost comically constructed juxtapositions of the levels of fiction, is a mode and perhaps even a condition the artist shares with his time.

Mindaugas Lukosaitis
1980 Born in Siaulai, lives and works in Siauliai, Vilnius, Lithuania

Education

1999-2004
Department of Sculpture, Vilnius Academy of Fine Arts, Lithuania

Solo Exhibition

2004
IBID Projects, Vilnius, Lithuania

Selected Group Exhibitions

2005
Milena Dragicevic and Mindaugas Lukosaitis, Galerie Fons Welters, Amsterdam, Netherlands
Spielräume, Wilhelm Lehmbruck Museum, Duisburg, Germany
Populism, Frankfurter Kunstverein, Frankfurt, Germany, Stedelijk Museum, Amsterdam, Netherlands, National Center of Art, Architecture and Design, Oslo, Norway and Contemporary Art Center, Vilnius, Lithuania
Alien Bodies, Prima Centar, Skopje, The Republic of Macedonia
Sao Paulo 26th Biennale, Sao Paulo, Brasil
In my own Juice, Rotermanni Soolaladu, Tallin, Estonia

2004
Who if not we...?, BAK, Utrecht and Centraal Museum, Utrecht, Netherlands

2003
2 show, CAC, Contemporary Art Center, Vilnius, Lithuania

2002
International Festival of Performance, Helsinki, Finland
Nr. 2, Akademija Gallery, Vilnius, Lithuania

2000
After the Wall, Moderna Museet Stockholm, Sweden

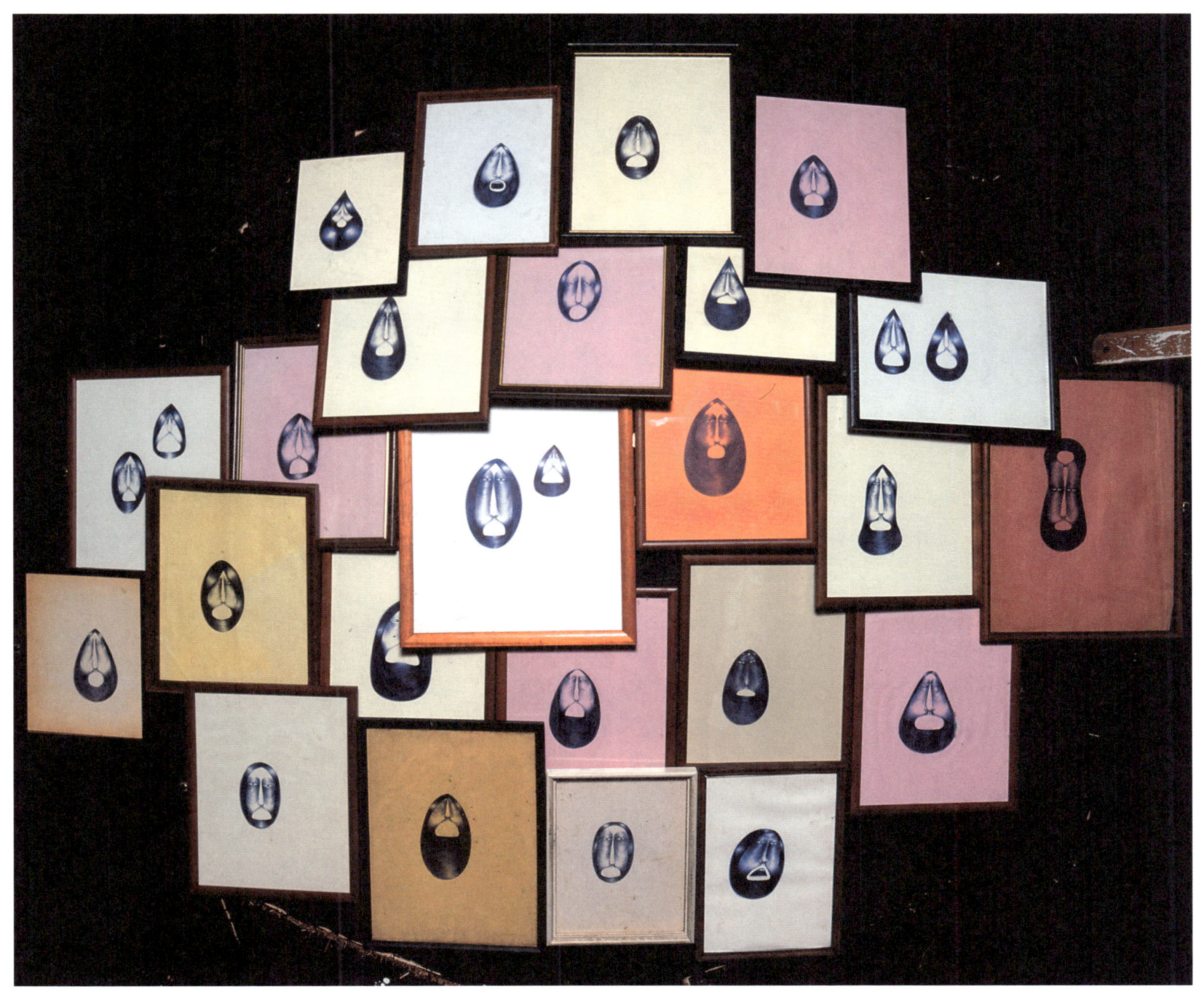

Untitled. 2005

Barry McGee
Born 1966 San Francisco, USA. Lives and works in San Francisco.

Education

1991
B.F.A., Printing and printmaking, San Francisco Art Institute, CA, USA

Selected Solo Exhibitions

2005
Easy Tonto, Modern Art Inc., London, UK
One More Thing, Deitch Projects, NY
Things Are Really Getting Better, Museum Het Domein Sittard, Netherlands

2004
John Kaldor Projects: Barry McGee, Metropolitan Meat Market Arts hub, North Melbourne, Australia
Barry McGee, Rose Art Museum, Brandeis University, Waltham MA
Deitch Projects, NY

2002
Prada Foundation, Milan, Italy
Modern Art Inc., London, UK
Gallery Paule Anglim, San Francisco, CA, USA

2000
UCLA Hammer Museum, Los Angeles, CA, USA
Alleged Galleries, Tokyo, Japan

1999
The Buddy System, Deitch Projects, New York, NY, USA
Hoss, Rice University Art Gallery, Houston, TX, USA

1998
Regards, Walker Art Center, Minneapolis, MN, USA

Selected Group Exhibitions

2005
Beautiful Losers: Contemporary Art and Street Culture, Contemporary Museum, Baltimore, USA

2004
Monument to Now, The Dakis Joannou Colections Foundation, Athens, Greece
Beautiful Losers: Contemporary Art, Skateboarding, and Street Culture, Contemporary Arts Center, Cincinnati, USA
Barry McGee and Josh Lazcano, Gallery Paule Anglim, San Francisco, USA

2003
Ten by Twenty, Yerba Buena Center for the Arts, San Francisco, CA, USA
A Way With Words, John Berggruen Gallery, San Francisco, CA, USA
Outerspace Hillbilly, The Luggage Store, San Francisco, CA, USA
Session the Bowl, Deitch Projects, New York, USA

2002
The Broken Down Mysterious Doors Of The Impossible, Lump Gallery, Raleigh, N.C., USA
Drawing Now: Eight Propositions, Museum of Modern Art, New York, USA
Liverpool Biennial, Liverpool, UK

2001
Holdfast, Barry McGee and Margaret Kilgallen, Deste Foundation, Centre for Contemporary Arts, Athens, Greece
Un Art Populaire, Fondation Cartier pour l'art contemporain, Paris, France
Venice Biennale, Venice, Italy
Widely Unknown, Deitch Projects, New York, USA

2000
Street Market, Parco Gallery, Tokyo, Japan
Street Market, Deitch Projects, New York, USA
Made in California, Los Angeles County Museum of Art, CA, USA
Indelible Market, Institute of Contemporary Art, Philadelphia, PA, USA

1999
Robert Crumb, Phillip Guston, Barry McGee, Paul Morris Gallery, New York

Over and above the current status of graffiti as political by nature, Barry McGee's long-standing embrace of the genre is also grounded in a view of the creative effect of drawing as such; that is, the placing of signs as a primal and thus artistically fundamental activity; but with the crucial difference from the classic art of drawing that for McGee it is often not a white surface that forms the starting-point, but an architectural setting, and old signboard, some cheap coloured paper from the nearest copy-shop, an everyday object like a car, or a mixture of all of this. Or, as he himself has put it, "the sensory overload of urban street life".

The distinction between the found and the invented, but for the artist in particular the fusion of the two, is essential and can be decoded at all levels by McGee's work. It is only there, in an always revolving practice, it still makes sense for him to engage in art, which once more reflects his point of departure in the radically public character of graffiti. Only thus, in his view, can art sustain its ability and freedom to talk back to the world. And that means among other things "anything that's not mainstream America".

The *Biro drawings*, whose practice goes back several years, also form part of other contexts, typically iconostasis-like accumulations of photographs and drawings. They are similarly installed one upon another with the emphasis on layers that is precisely what the practitioners of graffiti work with. As for the frames, they are also givens: they are mass-produced frames of the cheapest type, the paper is printing paper and the ballpoint pen is worth no more than a dime. Easy come, yes, but hardly so easy go! There is no doubt about the affinity with urban iconology with its home-made signs and practical solutions to elementary communication tasks. So, anti-lifestyle and more or less need-stimulating practices. But something else is also at play in these drawings, something that in a certain sense forms a bridge for McGee's practice between street art and high art. Nowhere in his work is the line – at once ritualized and sensitive – so radicalized in its use. It quite literally runs into itself with its endless soft curves of blue strokes that together form human faces in stages between masks and biological portraits. There is huge variation in the rhetorical tropes and a magic sensitivity to the characterful in the endless sea of impressions that the allegedly anonymous city face bears with it – in melancholy, in aggression and in apathy. It is not just a case of high-low issues in the lingo of art history. Barry McGee's lines have something to do with Matisse, just as graffiti has.

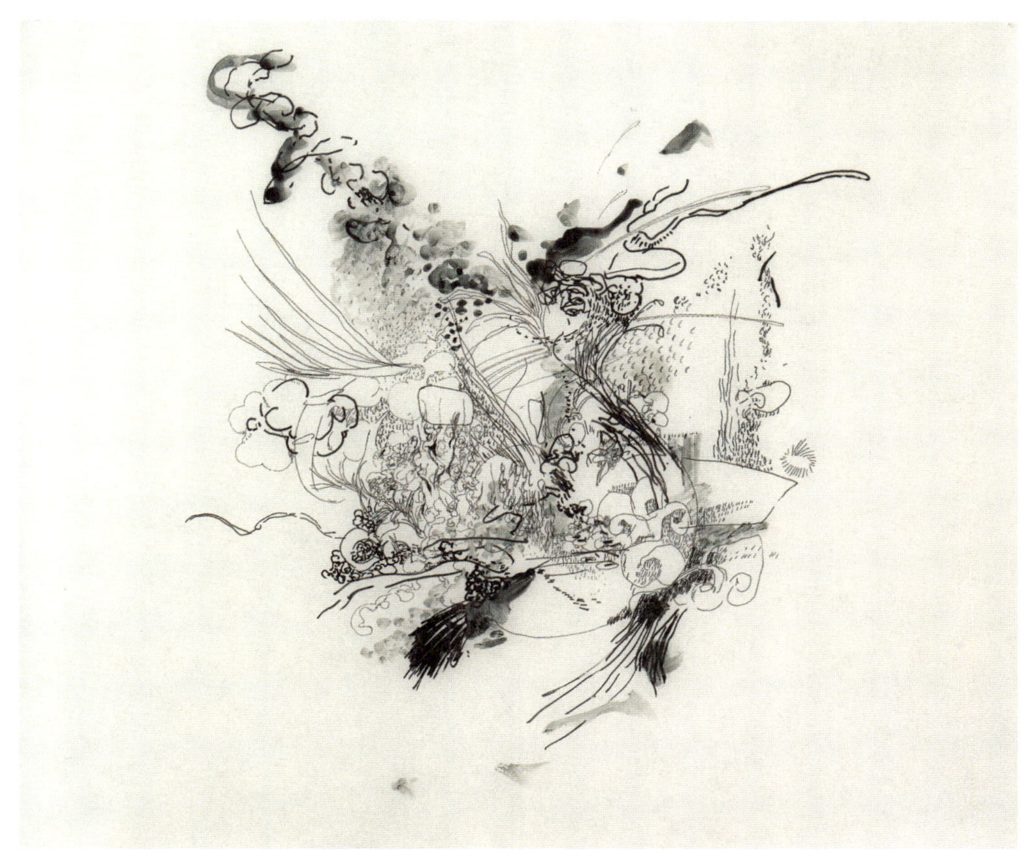

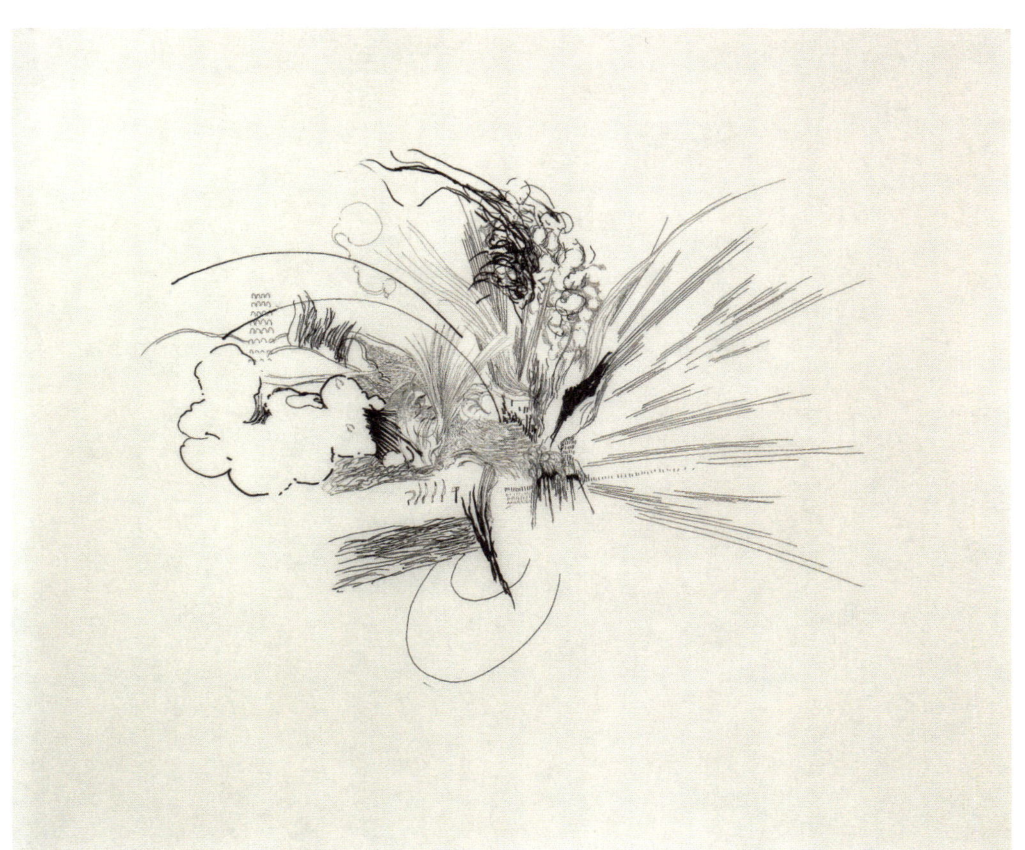

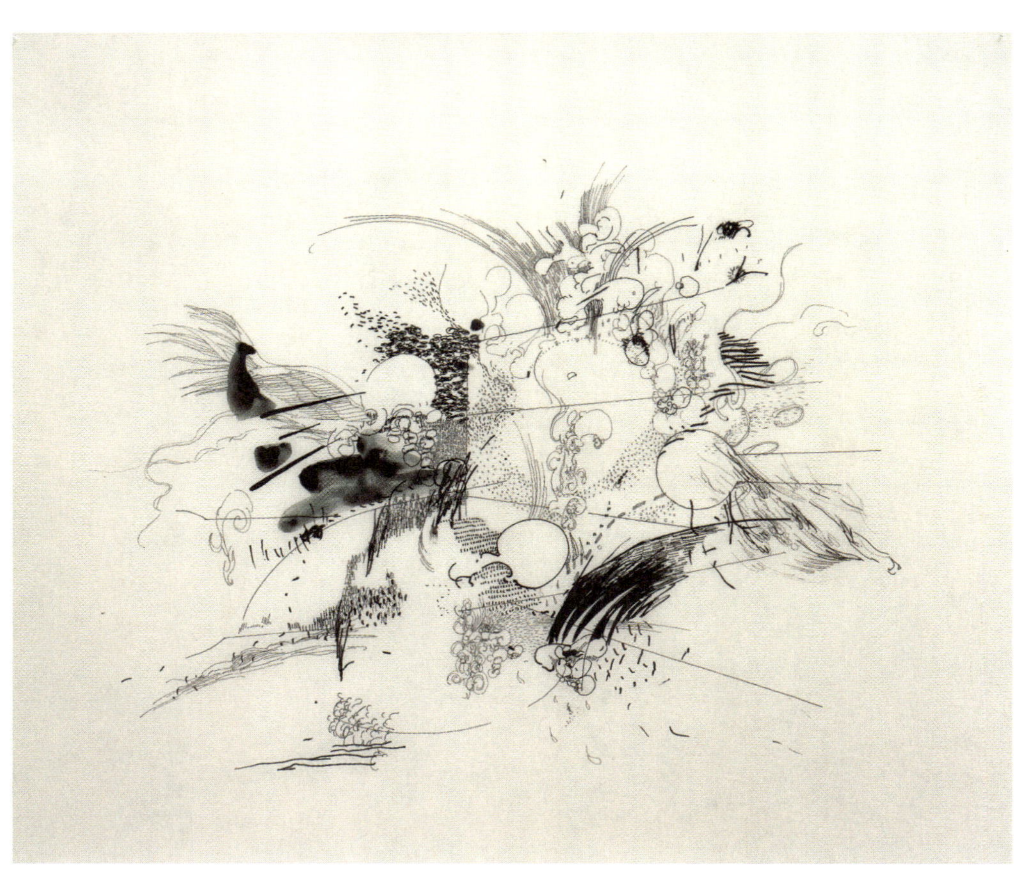

Untitled. 2002. **Untitled**. 2002. **Untitled**. 2002

Julie Mehretu
Born 1970, Addis Ababa, Ethiopia. Lives and works in New York, USA

Education

1997
MFA, Honours, Rhode Island School of Design
1992
BA, Kalamazoo College, Michigan
1991
University Cheik Anta Diop, Dakar, Senegal

Selected Solo Exhibitions

2005
The Project, New York, NY
Currents 95: Julie Mehretu, Saint Louis Art Museum, USA
Julie Mehretu: Drawing into Painting, Gallery at Redcat, Los Angeles, USA

2004
Julie Mehretu – Matrix 211: Manifestation, Berkeley Art Museum, USA
Julie Mehretu: Drawing into Painting, Albright-Knox Art Gallery, Buffalo, NY

2003
Galerie Anne De Villepoix, Paris, France
Carlier | gebauer, Berlin, Germany
Julie Mehretu: Drawing into Painting, Walker Art Center, MN

2002
White Cube, London, UK

2001
The Project, New York, NY
Art Pace, San Antonio, TX

Selected Group Exhibitions

2005
Baroque and Neobaroque, Domus Artium 2002, Salamanca, Spain
Remote Viewing (Invented Worlds in Recent Painting and Drawing), The
Whitney Museum, New York, USA
Africa Remix, Museum Kunstpalast, Düsseldorf, Germany
Mythologies, Walker Art Center, Minneapolis, USA

2004
Africa Remix, Hayward gallery London, UK; Centre Pompidou, Paris, France
Whitney Biennial, The Whitney Museum of American Art, New York, USA
Sao Paulo Biennial, Sao Paulo, Brazil

2003
Poetic Justice, 8th International Istanbul Biennial, Istanbul, Turkey
The Moderns, Castello di Rivoli Museum of Contemporary Art, Turino, Italy
GNS, Palais du Tokyo, Paris, France
Prague Biennale 1, Prague, The Czech Republic
Splat Boom Pow!, Contemporary Arts Museum, Houston, USA

2002
Drawing Now: Eight Propositions, Museum of Modern Art, New York, USA
Out of Site, New Museum, New York, USA
Stalder-Mehretu-Solakov, Kunstmuseum Thun, Switzerland
Centre of Attraction, The 8th Baltic Triennial of International Art, Vilnius,
Lithuania
The Busan Biennale, Busan, Korea
*Terra Incognita: Contemporary Artists' Maps and Other Visual Organizing
Systems*, Contemporary Arts Museum, St. Louis, MO, USA

2001
Urgent Painting, Musee d'Art Moderne de la Ville de Paris, Paris, France
The Americans, Barbican Art Centre, London, UK
Painting at the Edge of the World, Walker Arts Center, Minneapolis, USA
Freestyle, Studio Museum in Harlem, New York, NY, USA
Casino 2001, Stedelijk Museum Voor Actuele Kunst, Gent, Belgium

2000
Selections Fall 2000, The Drawing Centre, New York, NY, USA
Five Continents and One City, Museo de la Ciudad de Mexico, Mexico City
Greater New York, P.S.1 Contemporary Arts Centre, New York, USA

Putting the world into the world – a critic has characterized the core of Julie Mehretu's artistic project in these words. The reference is not to a categorizing practice – something meant to procure order and manageability; on the contrary it is to something that at a different, more fundamental level testifies to the complexity of the world. Mehretu's works are both in the technical sense, as drawing practice, and as utterances about the world, a surgical intervention, a radically new body sewn together, with visible cæsuras and scar tissue as a result. A boundless and at the same time tacked-together world, which is why tattoos, with their particular iconographic coordinates, and superimposed as they are on the landscape of the skin, not surprisingly hold the interest of the artist.

The drawing practice of the artist unfolds in several categories, but often with no small affinities with her paintings. These often consist of several layers, and in this connection semi-transparent architectural paper – mylar and vellum – plays a crucial role. Translucence is essential to the content of the works; to a great extent they are generated by the idea of a membrane, which both holds something in and osmoses information from other strata. Paradoxically, it is precisely the traditional preferences of drawing and its special talent for the constructed and the conceptual outline that are pinned down by this new approach.

There are drawings which, almost in a classical sense, catalogue the whole vocabulary of the line, from point and stroke to gesture and dizzying network. Others co-exist with templates, more or less documentable topographies and plan-regulated architectural projections. And to this we must add – or perhaps rather, over this is embedded – the artist's own biographical trajectory, connecting places like Ethiopia, Michigan, Senegal and Rhode Island. A third type, with the demonstrative authority of the light-box, approaches the public space that has traditionally, and as institutional practice, been something utterly other than drawing as a medium.

The multitude of perspectives, scales and strata are thus not only charged with references to the history of art and architecture; they are also statements about human presence past, present and future. Delving a little into the matter of the time perspective in Mehretu's works – and as a feature of drawing on the whole – one could regard her works not as excavations of the past, but as a kind of archaeology of the future; a synthetic phenomenon between historical and futuristic fictions, where it is the response and involvement of the viewer that more than anything else establishes the final chronology. In this non-hierarchical cultural geometry many of the structures and agendas overlap which, at the beginning of the 21st century, both inform us and at the same time seem to subject us to an almost unbearable osmotic pressure.

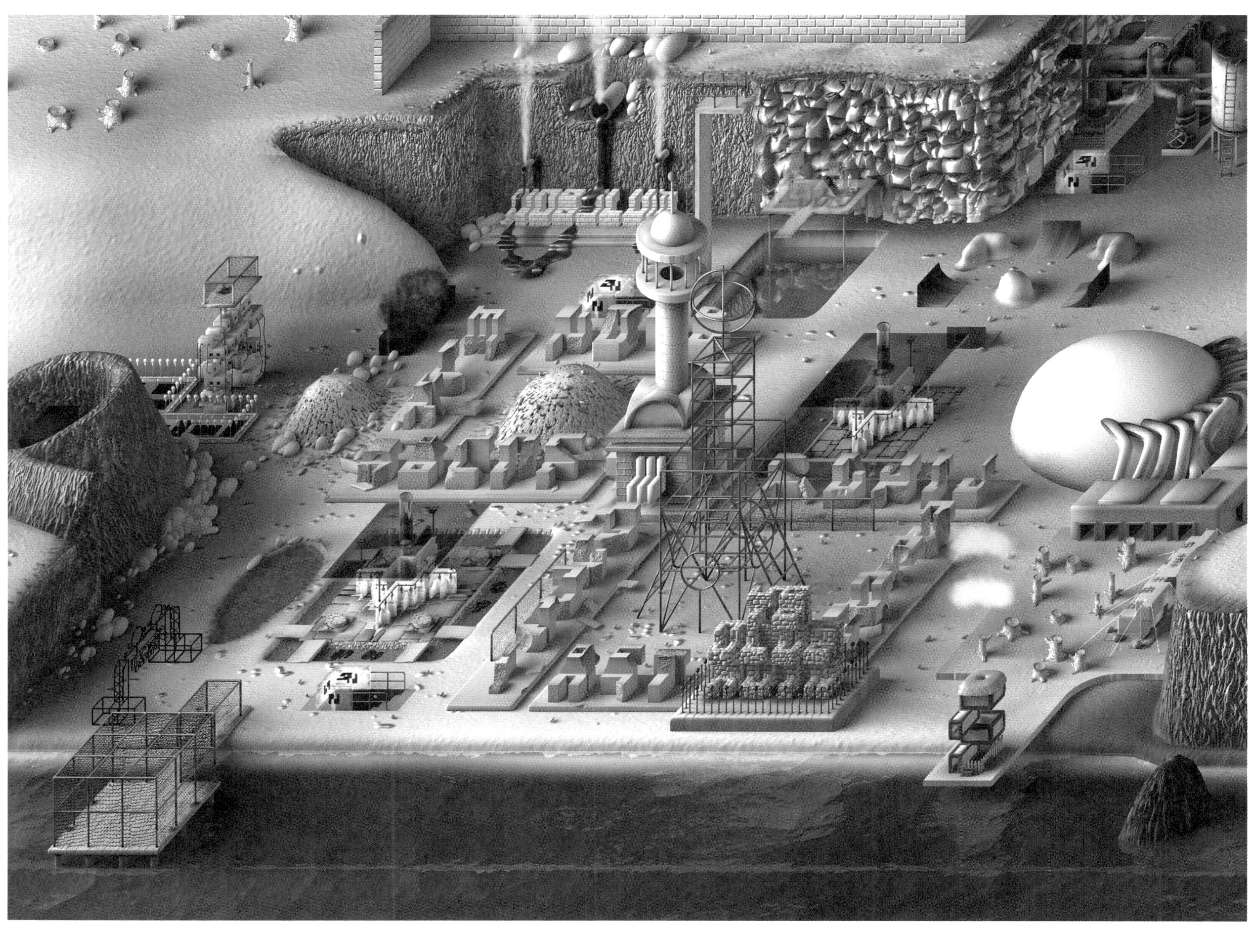

Paul Noble
Born 1963 in Dilston, Northumberland, UK. Lives and works in London

Education

1986
BA Fine Art at Humberside College of Higher Education

1983
Sunderland Polytechnic

Selected Solo Exhibitions

2005
Paul Noble, Migros Museum für Gegenwartskunst, Zürich, Switzerland
Paul Noble: No Accidents, Only Mistakes, Museum Boijmans Van
Beuningen, Rotterdam, Netherlands

2004
Paul Noble, Whitechapel Art Gallery, London, UK
Paul Noble, Maureen Paley, London, UK

2003
New Room of Contemporary Art, Paul Noble, Albright Knox Art Gallery,
Buffalo, New York, USA

2001
Unified Nobson, MAMCO, Geneva, Switzerland
Paul Noble: acumulus noblitatus, Maureen Paley Interim Art, London

Selected Group Exhibitions

2005
Ecstacy – In and About Altered States, MOCA The Geffen Contemporary,
Los Angeles, CA, USA
Monuments to the USA, CCA Wattis Institute for Contemporary Arts,
San Francisco, CA, USA

2004
Sodium and Asphalt - British Contemporary Art in Mexico, Museo de Arte
Contemporáneo, Monterrey, Mexico
Biennale of Sidney 2004, Biennial Sydney, Australia
Motes in all eyes, The Ship. London, UK
Future Noir, Gorney Bravin + Lee, New York, USA

2003
8th International Istanbul Biennial - Poetic Justice, Istanbul Foundation for
Culture and Arts, Istanbul, Turkey
Bewitched, Bothered and Bewildered, Laznia Centre for Contemporary Art,
Danzig, Poland and Migros Museum für Gegenwartskunst, Zürich, Switzerland
Independence, South London Gallery, London, UK
Living Inside the Grid, New museum of Contemporary Art, New York, USA
Days Like These: Tate Triennial of Contemporary British Art, Tate Britain, London, UK

2002
FACE/OFF: a Portrait of the Artist, Kettle's Yard, Cambridge, UK
(The World May Be) Fantastic, The Biennale of Sidney
Drawing now: eight propositions, The Museum of Modern Art, New York, USA
Paul Noble and Giovanni Battista Piranesi, Susan Inglett, New York, USA

2001
By Hand: Pattern, Precision and repetition in Contemporary Drawing, University Art Museum,
California State University, Long beach, USA

2000
Manifesta 3 Ljubljana 2000, International Foundation Manifesta, Amsterdam, Netherlands

1999
Abracadabra: International Contemporary Art, Tate, London, UK

1998
A to Z, The Approach, London, UK
Paul Noble: Nobson, The Chisendale Gallery, London, UK
Surfacing, contemporary drawing, ICA, London, UK

1997
Belladonna, ICA, London, UK

The prison-house of language as Michel Foucault has described it is one of the things that comes to mind when one is confronted with Noble's drawings – once one has got used to the generic anomaly. For in format they often resemble tapestries more than hand drawings; they stretch far beyond the bodily span that is still mainly associated with the medium. In Noble's works the letters, the basic architectural elements of language, can also be viewed concretely as houses and residences. To that end the artist has developed on the computer the typeface *Nobfont*, whose characteristic feature is a consistent three-dimensionality in the rendering, and which in reality incorporates a critique of modernism's inhuman concrete housing – in language, 'so to speak'. And the choice of drawing as medium is in that context a political statement in itself.

Since 1991 Noble has worked with a project dealing with the city of 'Nobson', its suburbs and environs: The beaches, the fields and the sea. Elevated above reality, certainly; but in its projection of some of the main themes of the twentieth century – urbanity, territorial boundaries and ecological sustainability – it is at the same time a project that lets its searchlights scan the horizons of the future. Yet it will never become a traditional futuristic project; the works exhibit their own decay too clearly for that. For Noble the temporal dimension is not so easily frozen.

The perception of the works – from bird's-eye view to close-up scrutiny – is only one of their inherent dichotomies. The world is not good, that is clear enough. The great grid surrounds us and in many ways dictates our behaviour – rather as in Pink Floyd's *The Wall*, and here too Orwellian in character and pervasiveness. But at the same time Noble's world is edifying: as a Babel-like parable it contributes to the discussion of a number of the big issues on the cultural agenda. It is about how we arrange our life and society as a whole. And the argument turns on a knife-edge between determined political pessimism – Noble himself lived in derelict buildings in London during the Thatcher era – and typical Anglo-Saxon humour that does not hesitate to physicalize and carnivalize the world where the flow of sludge and faeces constantly enriches and engulfs any tendency towards clean surfaces. In itself an interesting situation for a draughtsman. After all, his basic premise is the purity of the paper versus the deposited trace of the line. At the level of content, what we encounter here is a basic scepticism about the power of the word – as in treaties and lines on maps. Modernism isn't dead, it just smells funny.

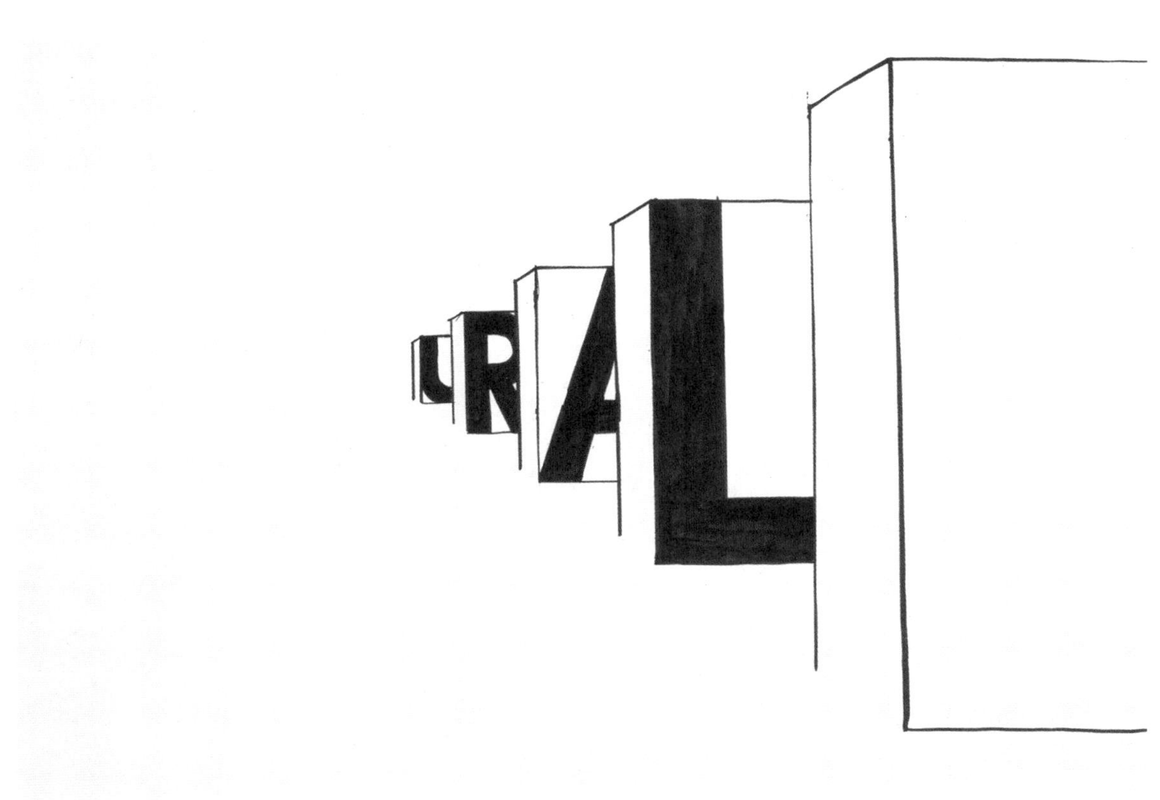

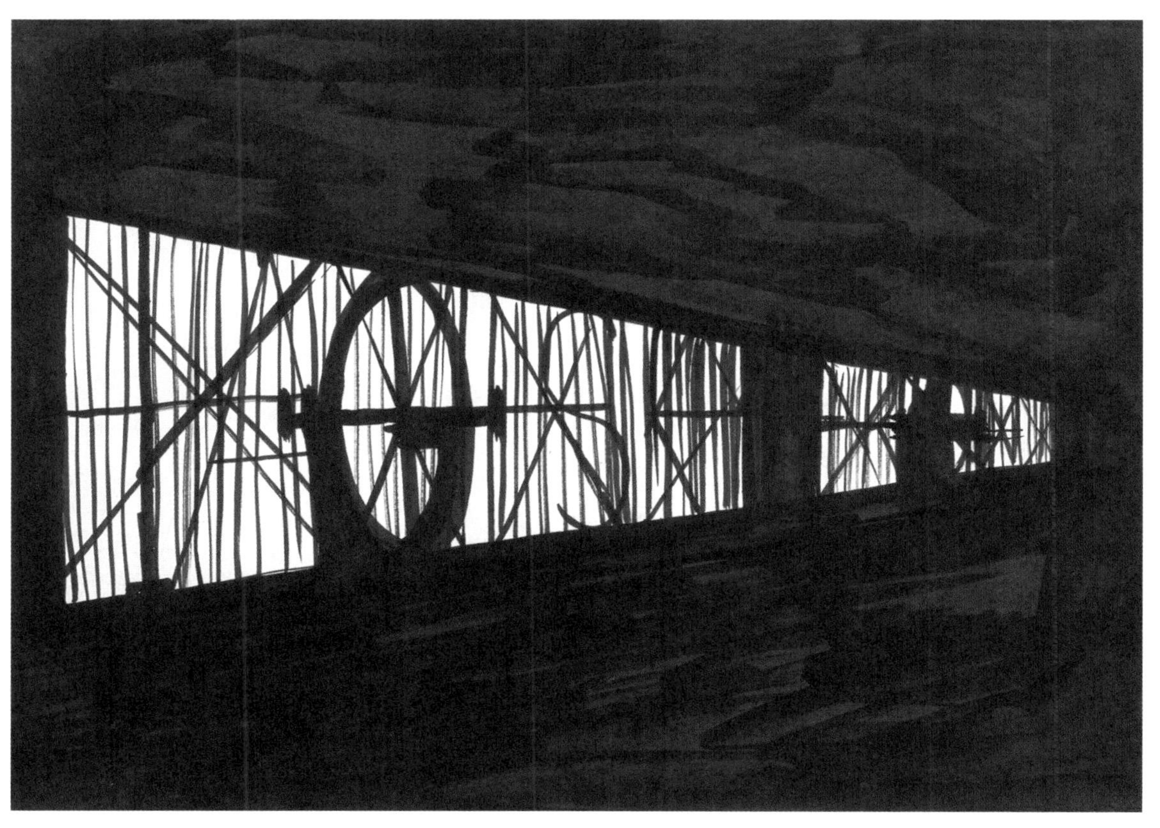

Wilhelm Sasnal
Born 1972, Tarnow, Poland. Lives and works in Tarnow.

Selected solo Exhibitions

2005
Wilhelm Sasnal, Anton Kern Gallery, New York, USA
Wilhelm Sasnal, Chinati Foundation / Judd Foundation, Marfa, TX, USA

2004
Wilhelm Sasnal: The Band, Galerie Hauser & Wirth, Zürich, Switzerland
Anton Kern Gallery, New York, USA
Camden Arts Centre, London, England
Wilhelm Sasnal, Galerie Johnen + Schöttle, Cologne, Germany
Wilhelm Sasnal – Map Trap, Galerie Raster, Warsaw, Poland

2003
3 o'clock road block, Sadie Coles HQ, London, England
Wilhelm Sasnal, Contemporary Art, MUHKA, Antwerp, Belgium
Wilhelm Sasnal, Westfälischer Kunstverein, Münster, Germany
Anton Kern Gallery, New York, USA
Irit Sommer Galllery, Tel Aviv, Israel
Wilhelm Sasnal, Kunsthalle Zürich, Switzerland

2002
PHO, Galerie Johnen & Schöttle, Cologne, Germany
Show on your hands – Look – Come closer, Foksal Gallery Foundation,
Warsaw, Poland

2001
Cars and Men, Foksal Gallery Foundation, Warsaw, Poland
Everyday Life in Poland between 1999 and 2000, Galeria Raster, Warsaw,
Poland

2000
Board Game, Galeria Potocka, Cracow, Poland

Selected Group Exhibitions

2005
M Stadt / steirischer herbst, Kunsthaus Graz, Austria
It takes some time to open an oyster, Centro Cultural Andratx, Mallorca,
Spain
Prague Biennale 2, The Czech Republic
Reykjavik Arts Festival 2005, Iceland
What's New, Pussycat, Neuerwerbungen und Sammlung Ströher, Museum
für Moderne Kunst, Frankfurt, Germany

2004
The Triumph of Painting, Saatchi Gallery, London, UK
Funny Cuts, Staatsgalerie Stuttgart, Germany
Biennale São Paulo 2004, Brasil
Some Forgotten Place, Berkeley Art Museum, Berkeley, CA, USA
From Above, Georg Kargl, Vienna, Austria
Collection Summer 2004, Museum van Hedendaagse Kunst, Antwerpen,
Belgium
Under the White and Red Flag – New Art From Poland, Contemporary Art
Center, Vilnius, Lithuania

2003
Creeping Revolution 2, Roseum, Malmö, Sweden
Wilhelm Sasnal & Monika Sosnowska, Galleria Laura Pecci, Milan, Italy
4ever Young, Sommer Contemporary Art, Tel-Aviv, Israel

2002
After Reality - Painting on the Move, Kunsthalle Basel, Switzerland
Pause, 4th Gwangju Biennial, Gwangju, South Korea
Urgent Painting, Musée d'art moderne de la Ville de Paris, Paris, France

2001
Painters' Competition, Galeria Bielska BWA, Bielsko-Biala, Poland
1st Tirana Biennial, Tirana, Albania
Bureaucracy, Foksal Gallery Foundation, Warsaw, Poland

2000
Scena 2000, CCA Ujazdowski Castle, Warsaw, Poland
100% Painting, BWA Gallery, Poznan, Poland

The black-and-white scale in Sasnal's ink drawings is devoid of grey shades. Nevertheless his register is subtly able to modulate the perception of the seen in a number of directions – as rich as in his paintings, just as ostensibly anonymous and beyond what one would normally describe as *focus*. All the same the extreme graphic effects of the works assume a kind of authority at arm's length.

The variation in the exhibited drawings is characteristic of the mode in which Sasnal generally operates. There are many perspectives and one senses many, partly historical interfaces. The place and objects of everyday life are brought forth in a process where the viewer fully accepts not having chosen the angle of view. This is obviously the artist's, and yet – as is strikingly often the case in art now – one is in a certain sense also in the picture oneself. One can only respond to this consistently non-judgemental point of departure by engaging oneself. That's how it works. The viewer is involved in the artist's own ambivalence about and to some extent mistrust of the image. Sasnal's pointed presence – in drawing as well as painting – becomes the device which at once stresses the legitimacy of the solo performance and the indispensability of teamwork in the production of meaning. It is like the individual pages of a diary: everything is possible and everything possible takes place, but it is inevitably read as a totality.

Sasnal interferes with the registers in our knowledge and our vision that link the world with its image. Between the object and its representation, to use the philosophical terminology. There is a strange, involved boredom at play between what appear to be very important components of existence; of the artist's own life, one is tempted to think, since he also seizes on the world's more intimate banalities: a pedestrian tunnel, a table, some rather claustrophobic little spaces, and something that looks like Hollywood lettering – placed not on the heights around Los Angeles, but as architecturally designed blocks at a locality that may or may not have something to do with the Ural Mountains. But with a distinctly different effect from Ed Ruscha's cooler parallel universe. Or the date 1957 in mirror-writing, leaving a sense of authority that might well be crucial to the reading, but might also only tend to further obscure the focus.

The black and white areas do not stand starkly against each other in the traditional graphic way: they generate and also presuppose each other. Within the *noir* of the ink live innumerable expressions and impressions, just as white – demarcated by black – lives in Sasnal's drawing as *line*. The artist has been quoted several times as feeling unusually susceptible to pictures, and his drawings in particular testify to this – no matter whether the source of the work is photographic or whether it originates in episodic, private events.

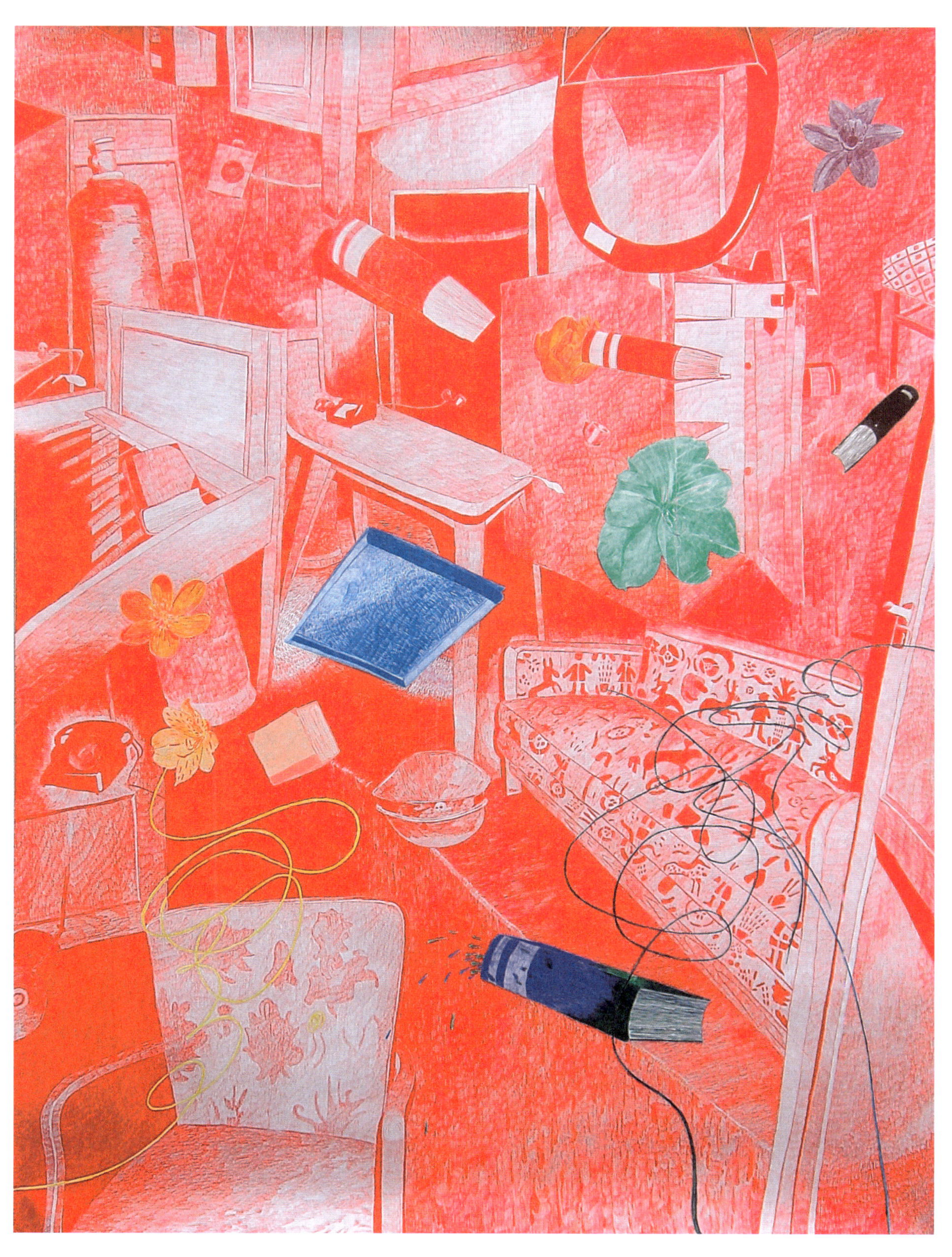

Morten Schelde

Clearly, the extremely laborious conversion of a photographic original into massive quantities of red-crayon shading already in itself makes the time factor tangible, but there is also an intended slowness in Morten Schelde's works that tries to stem the ubiquitous rush of the information flow.

Schelde's red world is in a way private. There is a confessional element in the work which in many respects attunes it to the artistic output of many of his contemporaries, but it does not associate it with a definable culture – *sub-* or otherwise; it does not have the character of sociological (self-) investigation, nor does it swell the neo-Utopian wave. The reporting of the seen is thus not only genuine enough, it is the prime cause of the works. And when bodily functioning is factored in with the ritual, febrile shading of the white surface with the coloured crayon, the spaces and places are scoured out of the systems of which they normally form a part. Sometimes even on to the walls of the institution. Not that they are isolated from the world; rather, what emerge are grudgingly exposed connections and paths *to* the world. *Children of Suburbia* – the title of the artist's evolving production of drawings over the past few years – is a world system, a world-picture in a certain sense, that of spatters of instamatic moments, with all the ramifications and cultural breadth this involves.

The motifs in Schelde's art are communicated from the medium itself, from the photograph, via personal experience and into a space of the imagination that is hyper-real – pure fiction, and thus open to the viewer. The photographic awareness we carry with us includes the individual through successions of coded gazes. From the language of film, for example, but also from the pioneering expeditions of childhood, we come to know the marked through what is in every way ordinary: the suburban road, not the spectacular motorway junction; the trees, not the city parks; the paths, not the boulevards; the airports instead of the skylines and the great urban prospects. That is, all the after-echoes of modernity and highly unspectacular directions offered to the gaze. A kind of panoramic backstage – to include all the visual orientations and at the same time point to some of the artist's motifs from garages and back stairs.

Morten Schelde
Born 1972 in Copenhagen, Denmark. Lives and works in Berlin, Germany

Education

2001
The Royal Danish Academy of Fine Arts, Copenhagen
1996
The Academy of Fine Arts, Funen

Selected solo exhibitions

2005
Morten Schelde, Arnstedt & Kullgren, Östra Karup, Sweden

2003
The End of Dinosaurs, Overgaden, Copenhagen, Denmark
Shadows dream of Light, griedervonputtkamer, Berlin, Germany

2002
Children of Suburbia III, Gustaf Gimm, Copenhagen, Denmark

2001
Doppel 7, with Gabriela Albergaria, Galerie Kamm, Berlin, Germany

2000
Children of Suburbia, Kunstakademiet, Copenhagen, Denmark

Selected group shows

2005
Beate Gütschow/Morten Schelde, Kunstbank, Berlin, Germany
Milk, DCA Gallery, New York, USA
Saturday Morning, Josee Bienvenu Gallery, New York, USA
They call us lonely when we're really just alone, Vane Gallery, Newcastle, UK

2004
Das Böse, Guardini Stiftung, Berlin
Idyll – anti idyll, Subspace, Berlin, collaborate works with Gabriela Albergaria, Germany
Papierarbeiten von Männern, Oliver Croy's apartment in Berlin, Germany
Zwischenwelten, Haus Esters, Krefelder Kunstmuseen, Germany
Ind imellem, Galleri Tom Christoffersen, Copenhagen, Denmark

2003
60 artists, Pugh-Pugh, Berlin, Germany
Berlin Artfair I Griedervonputtkamer, Germany
Three reasons to be Cheerful, Secret West, Berlin, Germany
A Room of One's Own # I – IV, collaborate works with Gabriela Albergaria.
Maus Habitos, Casa das Artes, Porto, Portugal

2002
Let's crystallize, collaborate work with Gabriela Albergaria, Sparwasser HQ, Berlin, Germany
Esplanaden 2002, Charlottenborg, Copenhagen, Denmark

2001
EXIT 2001, Kunstforeningen, Copenhagen, Denmark

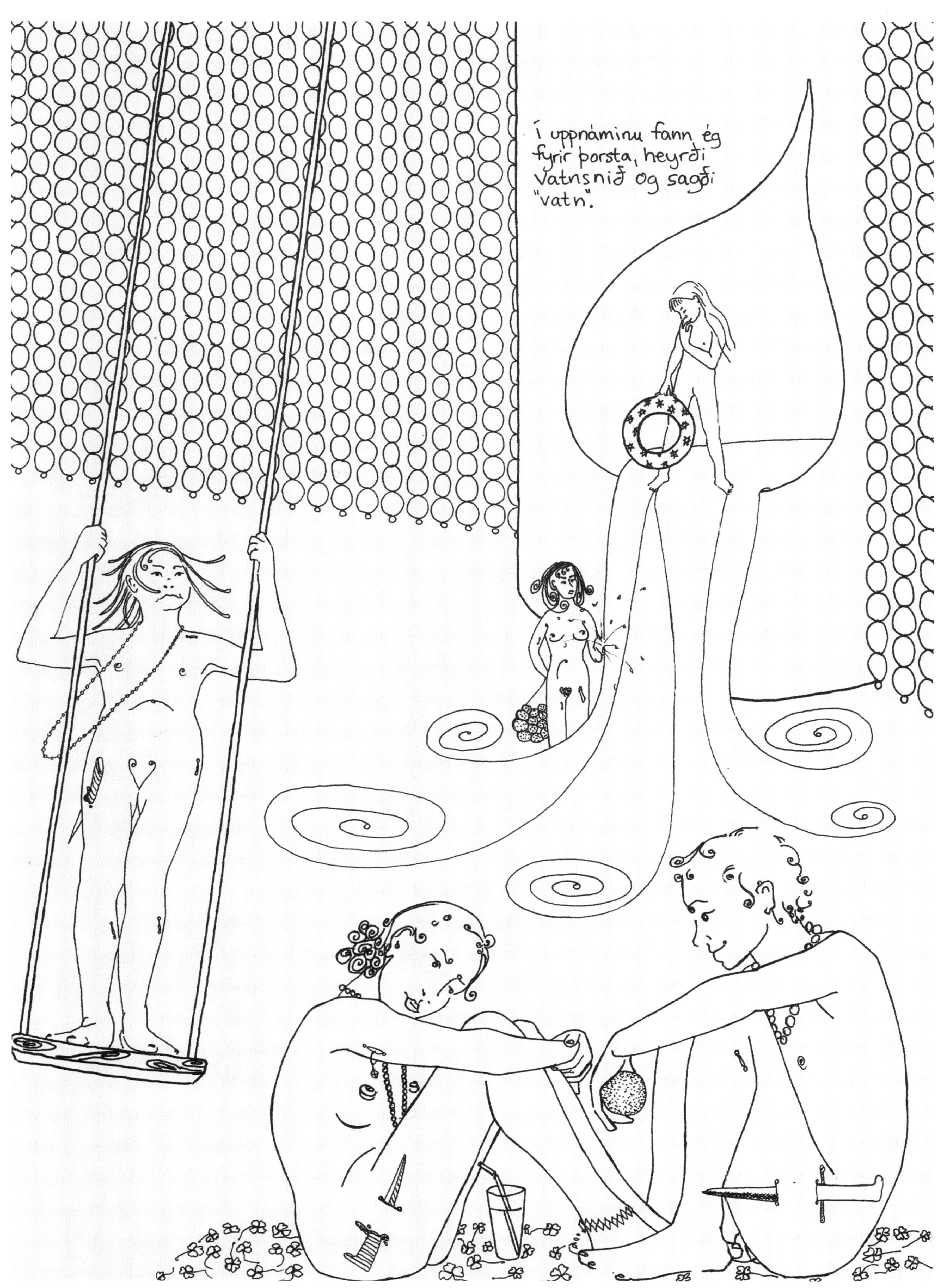
Í uppnáminu fann ég
fyrir þorsta, heyrði
vatnsnið og sagði
"vatn".

Inga Svala Thorsdottir

The exhibited works are all manifestations of the artist's work with a phenomenon that is also a place and bears the name BORG. The word is Icelandic for town, and goes back to the first settlements on the island back in the ninth century. The place even has its own coordinates: 21°W, 64°N, a precise topos for the ouk-topos of artistic expression. All that can be said about conditions at the locality is played out between pure Utopia and what, with a nod to another Nordic artist, Asger Jorn, can perhaps best be described as "luck and chance". All ideas of BORG start on the blank white surface. In the twentieth century the concepts of Utopia and settlement were closely associated with the projects of modernism and – when, as with BORG, we are talking about a megapolis – its often daunting attempt to create a cohesive everything out of nothing with new materials, for the greater common good of humanity. But as long as nothing more can be found at the coordinates than the Icelandic landscape, the place is a place of the mind, a projection – and in this there are ironically enough considerable similarities with the great revolutionary missions; but action is also associated with the power of the imagination. The artist has been there physically, in that sense something has taken place, so even though the processual logic of the artwork is unclear, this state of affairs has a meaning, also as an offshoot from the tradition of conceptual art, and not least its particular wrestling with the (non)material status of the work of art. Richard Long's documentation of travels through more or less accessible regions, and Robert Smithson's land art, for example. But the functional aspect is absent, which makes the works of Thorsdottir wilder and more romantic excursions from reality in the direction of luck and chance.

Through the widely differing manifestations of BORG runs the line, as a link with the central identity of the work: the thin ink line of the diary-like notes from the underground, with related sketches and the systematized sheaves of coloured strokes in the tinted landscape, but also cartography's myriads of abstract symbols and meteorology's printouts converted into large hatched diagrams in the manner of another Hamburg artist, Hanne Darboven. For Inga Svala Thorsdottir, the line is the instrument of the sketch, and the postulate in the analytical as well as the experimentally scanning and discursive sense. BORG is a place with a measurable number of sunshine hours a year, it is a sliver of the genesis of a thought – a *Geistesblick*, as it is called in German in the neurological research that also interests the artist – and it is the subjective artistic model for an international, spacious and by nature asymmetrical society.

Inga Svala Thórsdóttir
Born 1966, Iceland. Lives and works in Hamburg, Germany

Education

1991-1995
Hochschule für bildende Künste in Hamburg
1987-1991
Icelandic College of Arts and Crafts in Reykjavik

Selected Solo Exhibitions

2004
Standpunkt: Inga Svala Thórsdóttir, Hamburger Kunsthalle, Germany

2002
Borg / City, Hafnarhús/Reykjavík Art Museum, Reykjavík, Iceland
Borgaleidir, Pro qm, Berlin, Germany

2001
Bahnhof Reykjavik, Salon Beige, Berlin
Stars and Stripes, Bonner Kunstverein, Bonn, Germany
Thing's Right(s), New York, Ethan Cohen Fine Arts, New York, USA

1999
Thing's Right(s), Cuxhaven, Cuxhavener Kunstverein, Cuxhaven, Germany
Cuxhaven Badezimmer, Galerie Andreas Schulter, Hamburg, Germany
Vege-Pleasure Hong-Kong, Hanart TZ Gallery, Hong Kong, China
Eine Badewanne, Galerie Andreas Schlüter, Hamburg
Vitrinenglasschiebenfenster, Kunsthistorisches Institut der Universität Bonn,
Bonn, Germany

1998
Vege-Pleasure, Galleri I 8, Reykjavik Arts Festival, Iceland

Selected Group Exhibitions

2005
Wolfgang Hartman Preis, Kunstverein Ettlingen, Germany

2004
Tätig Sein, Neue Gesellschaft für Bildende Kunst, Germany

2003
vinyl sound scape, Ina Wudtke & Inga Svala Thorsdottir, Sprengel Museum,
Hannover, Germany
Unbuilt Cities, Kunstverein Bonn, Germany
Annette Wehrmann, Inga Svala Thorsdottir und Judith Hopf, Künstlerhaus
Stuttgart, Germany
Ina Wudtke & Inga Svala Thorsdottir, Sprengel Museum, Hannover,
Germany

2002
Weisse Jacke, Agentur für zeitgenössische Kunst, Hamburg, Germany
Ökonomien der Zeit, Akademie der Künste, Berlin, and Museum Ludwig,
Cologne, Germany
Wie konnte das Einhorn die Sintflut überstehen?, Neues Museum Weimar,
Germany

2001
II Bienal Mercosul, Porto Alegre, Brasil
Birnen, Bohnen & Speck, Shanghai Museum, Shanghai, China
Ferdafuda, Slunkaríkí, Ísafirdi, Iceland

2000
Lauf der Dinge, Kunsthalle Manege, St. Petersburg, Russia
Continental Shift, Musée d'Art Moderne et d'Art Contemporain de la Ville de
Liège, Belgium
Heimat Kunst, Haus der Kulturen der Welt, Berlin, Germany
En Dehors des Cartes, Centre Regional D'art Contemporain, Sete, France

Our House – in the flow of drawings

by Anders Kold

You would have to be more than ordinarily dismissive of the contemporary art scene to miss the fact that drawing as a genre is everywhere; either in the small format or with the whole volume of the installation, sometimes in combination with painting and photography. Apparently drawing can do anything. And in the course of my deliberations on the phenomenon 'drawing now' I happened on a text about contemporary painting that seemed to me to confirm at least one possible explanation of why the denizens of the art world have almost been vying with one another to show drawings in recent years. The author of the article, J.J. Charlesworth, describes the dominant relativistic characteristics of a period in which *"the claim that knowledge and reason might provide an objective, universal understanding of the world is seldom made, and in which a multitude of positions proliferate precisely because they make no claim to general legitimacy. In other words, nothing is prohibited because nothing can be said to be untrue"*.[1] In other words I think that the present popularity and dominance of the drawing is inextricably bound up with the factors that can be said to apply to the visual arts as a whole, here and now. The question then becomes whether we can still point to something that is specific to the drawing – and doesn't simply apply to everything?

So is there still anything special to be said *on line*? Or is the emancipation of drawing, if that is what we are witnessing, grounded in the fact that today it (simply) can and may do anything the other media can? Has drawing, in what could be called its new, extended field, simply become a medium that does not require its own, different kind of investment? And is this why, as Laura Hoptman states in the catalogue of MoMa's big exhibition *Drawing Now* in 2002, drawing is no longer defined only in terms of form, finish and manner of execution? [2] Clearly it has moved too far from its earlier status as processual documentation in the 1960s and 1970s for this to be true; nor does it primarily function any longer as a sketch for other, more finished media. And its famous modernist party piece as a medium and an activity that offers us a particular kind of insight into the artist's work, a special closeness and authenticity, does not seem to work either. It has lost its innocence.

The drawings of contemporary art, as they present themselves in the exhibition, are obviously constructs, concluded in character, consummated. They are not in the process of becoming, they make up their own worlds that offer the viewer empathy and identification. Often the time of the drawings is also the time of the viewer – brief, or protracted and developed, but manageable. For drawing still characteristically performs no tricks or modifications that escape our notice as observers. And it is here, in the relation between artwork and viewer, that the new drawing, the drawing of contemporary art, often breaks out of the conventional framework and our notions of the medium: the intimate format is far from being a guideline any more, and serial form often makes its appearance at the expense of the unique statement. Ernesto Caivano's and Paul Noble's mega-works bear witness to the drawing process at one extreme; Wilhelm Sasnal's reticent emphases do so at the other. Slow developments, panoramic sequences or staccato, filmic leaps with this very discontinuity as their point, are all factors that in a significant way have something to do with formats and extent. One speaks of drawings, not of the art of drawing, and the intimacy of the Print Room is no longer the natural point of departure.

At all events it should be clear that there are no anxieties about association with drawing today. As a by-product of the struggle of the avant-garde throughout the twentieth century, the hierarchies associated with genres and stages in the practice of the visual arts, which for centuries have granted the drawing a particular fixed significance as direct preparation, as the outline of an idea or as a privileged preview of the finished work, can no longer be said to apply with any certainty. Alongside this absence of contact anxiety, drawing in its new role – as the goal of its own existence – is perhaps not burdened as much as painting is by any anxiety of *experience*. As Emma Dexter interprets it, it is not only in contact with the underprivileged as subject, it has also been undervalued and undertheorized.[3] And as a further consequence of this it has not endlessly been declared dead and resurrected – as painting has. The question is whether one can also say that 'drawing now' has made its entry on the scene just at a time when the medium is no longer covered with labels like 'Old Europe', 'postwar American' or 'global'.

The starting-point for the exhibition and the choice of artists are based on tendencies that have been active in contemporary art for almost a decade now. So here I will permit myself, with the rationalization of hindsight, to recall how in 1999 I saw a series of 'Biro drawings' by the Danish artist Tal R for the first time, drawings of which I was unable to make head nor tail at the time. They showed phantom cities or alternative societies under the surface of the earth, equipped with hairdressers' salons, massage parlours, Kung Fu academies and rooms full of hookers and hookahs. And the exits led either to the city streets and eternal grill bars, or up unto something that was sympto-matically enough the artist's own back garden. What I had no sense of then was the dislocation of the works – indeed of the whole world – towards a place where things had not only been turned on their head, they were actually *inside* the head – of the artist, the viewer, the world. And in this state the world and the heads had been whirled away from any posited centre. A multiplicity of perspectives and asymmetries had been launched just at a time when art had quietly begun to shift away from ap-propriation and social sculpture towards a more privately motivated art. A hairdresser's salon was and is a world-model, a thought in a new kind of body, or, as the title of the present article suggests, quite simply a different architecture.

The drawn worlds of contemporary art thus ranges from illuminations of the historical past to images from magical excursions into the archaeology of the future. A flood of projections in time and space. And the supply routes into the works range from low-cultural and folkloristic resources like graffiti, posters and comics[4] over the many iconic images of film and the mass media to the more abstract instruments that take the measure of civilization: cartography, urban plans and architecture. It may sound obvious, but despite the great differences in the material, it is modernity – the notions and furnishings of the whole twentieth century – that is felt to be the locus of engage-ment. And perhaps one should give more attention to the insistent tone of this dialogue – not righteously indignant in the classic political style, but passionate, precisely be-cause it is personal; even when, as with Wilhelm Sasnal, an arm's-length authority is exercised with an extreme slowness in the telling, the private becomes public.

The house as an image of the basic human condition frames the material both metapho-ri-cally and quite concretely: our strivings and thoughts are manifested as architecture, one could say – in models that not surprisingly turn everything on its head. These are houses in motion, with bodies that extend into a kind of regionalism that is postmodern as Öyvind Fahlström's *Sketches for a World Map* from the 1970s was. In this connection it is truly thought-provoking that the afterbirth of modernism is still the urban with all the trimmings, not nature and the landscape. Depending on how politically one approaches the visual arts, one could say that with drawing, art is now exploiting undiscovered, repressed or suppressed resources. One could even consider whether drawing can be said to have won a new status as a part, although an aftershock, of the tidal wave that from the mid-1970s on swept women and other marginalized groups into the centre art.

From Inga Svala Thorsdottir's settlements, fixed at precise global coordinates in the vast Icelandic landscape, through Morten Schelde's panoramic views from a back-stage suburbia, to something as concrete as Barry McGee's "anything that's not main-stream America".[5] In opposition to the image of modernism – concretized as Orwellian models, planes and grids – innumerable spatiotemporal strata and alternative cultural geometries are outlined, all sharing the feature that the self is inscribed upon geogra-phy, history and architecture as yet another layer – in Julie Mehretu's universe another tattoo – across the white skin of the paper; and in Noble's case even all the way into the building-blocks of language. And how else for example is one to process history and collective memory in the absence of any documentary material, as Mindaugas Lukosaitis does with the Lithuanian resistance struggle? History – well, it materializes, not surprisingly, in a number of forms where fictionalization knows few bounds. Scenes are reshot, periods are spliced together, amazing encounters are arranged. Alongside the artist's more or less ironic self and gender, historical and mythological figures

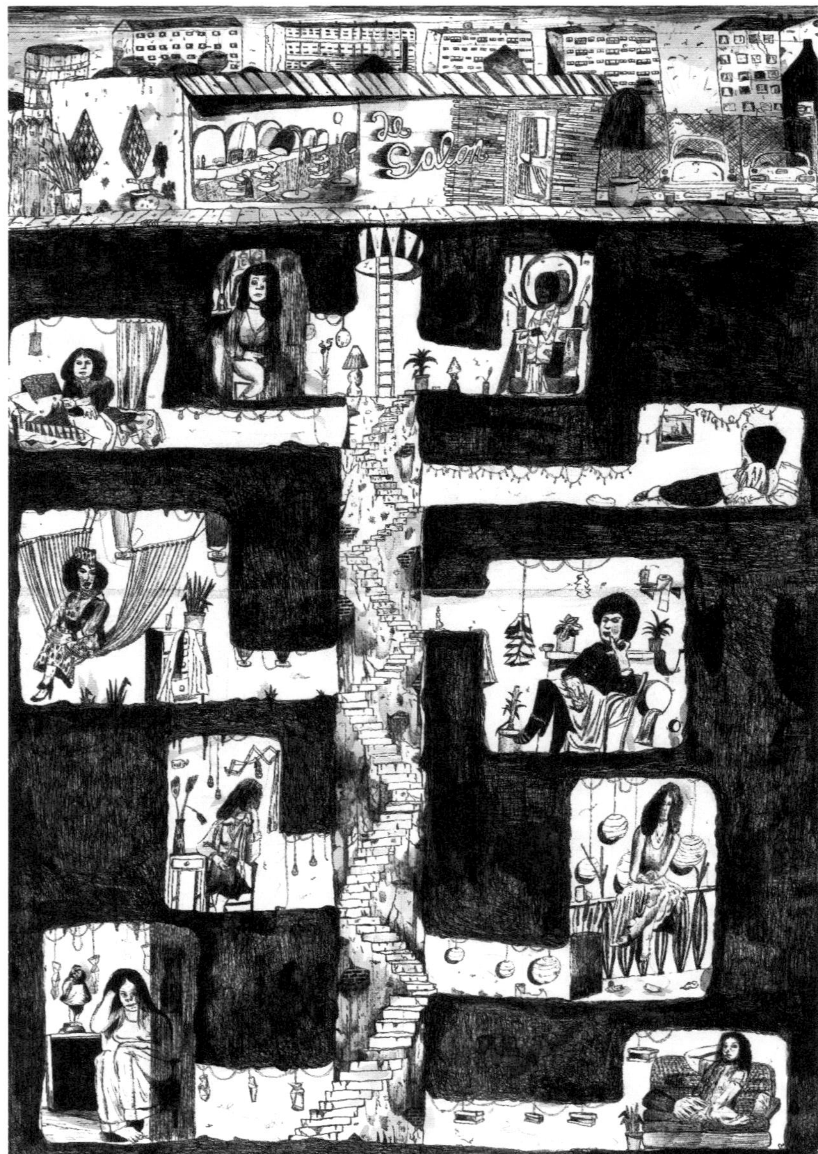

Tal R, **The Hairdresser**, 1999. Ballpoint on paper. 82,5 x 58 cm. Private collection, Courtesy Contemporary Fine Arts, Berlin. Photo: Jochen Littkemann

are inscribed in new scenarios far from Hollywood. And, as noted above, no one takes universal truths upon themselves.

So it should come as no surprise that the exhibited artists also do other things than draw. Several of them do not even have drawing as their primary medium. Drawing may be a spin-off from painting or video. This is essential to the characterization of the nature and practice of drawing right now; it means among other things that not all of them are great draughtsmen in the classic sense. And at the same time one can note that drawing is not only cultivated by women today, tracing their lines like fine needlework, while the men only draw (the) broad lines. In the classic relations between the genders, too, the drawing is well on its way to transcending its own and all sorts of conventions.

Neo-romantic or neo-conceptual, theoretical and discursive – or narrative and focused on the subjective? To a great extent it is all in play, spanning all the registers of contemporary art. In the end what can be said to remain the distinctive feature of drawing is its line-oriented, fundamentally narrative form; its ability to construct and stress the transforming and imaginative potential of the picture of the world. No other medium is able like drawing to mock up models of the well nigh insurmountable information leaps we encounter. There must be a reason, for example, why – across all known boundaries, including those of language – we send a drawing into orbit around the earth or use it as a therapeutic principle in connection with cases of child abuse. Drawing bears a potential as an interface with the other idioms of art. And this on the other hand answers the question whether 'drawing now' is a pocket of resistance in time, dedicated to slowness amidst the universal rush, or an outward-looking, inclusive practice.

Our house is being refurnished. There is activity on several floors at once. Not only above and below ground – between *high* and *low* – but also in the mix between abstraction and figuration and between phenomena at different but simultaneously active tempos. There are many paths to the drawing now, and despite all the maps, there is no atlas.

1. J.J. Charlesworth, *On Art's Permissive Society*, Modern Painters, p. 74, autumn 2004

2. Hoptman, *Drawing Now - Eight Propositions*, p. 167. The Museum of Modern Art, New York, 2002

3. Emma Dexter, *To Draw is to Be Human*, Vitamin D, p. 8. Phaidon Press, 2005

4. Hoptman, op.cit., p. 130. The Museum of Modern Art, New York, 2002

5. Barry McGee interviewed by Raphaela Platow, in *Barry McGee*, The Rose Art Museum of Brandeis University, unpaginated. 2004

LIST OF WORKS

Virginie Barré (b. 1970, France)

Women. 2005.
Femmes russes, 1917
Invitées à Buckingham Palace, 1919
Lady Emmeline Pethick-Lawrence, suffragette anglaise, 14-18
Saint-Moritz, 1924
Ann Scott James, journaliste, Angleterre, 1941
Greta Garbo
Robe à imprimé CND (campagne pour le désarmement nucléaire), 1967
Phyllis Gordon, Londres, 1939
Chamonix, 1925
Forestières, 1918
Michelle Tucker, mannequin, 197115 : Chamonix, 1925
Mrs Albu, Angleterre, années 1900
Hôtesses du British Rail's Advanced Passenger Train, 1972
Elsa Schiaparelli
Bee Jackson, championne du monde de charleston, années 20
Jane Fonda contre la guerre au Vietnam, Washington, 1970
1918
Dame Ethel Mary Smyth, compositeur et suffragette anglaise, 14-18
Baltimore, années 20
Amelia Earhart, aviatrice, USA, 1928
Mrs Kyle, années 1900
Bond Street, 39-45
Amy Johnson, aviatrice anglaise, 1936
Portières de Selfridges, Londres, 1915
Mrs Hepburn, Angleterre, années 1900
Marguerite Radclyff Hall, écrivain et lady Una Trowbridge, 1927
Coco Chanel
Années 30
Katharine Hepburn, 1952
Elsa Schiaparelli, 1931
Italiennes du Partito d'Azione
Londres, 1933
USA, 1929
Bowling en pyjama, années 30
Equipe de football, Londres, 14-18

35 computer drawings
Lambda print on paper
Edition 1/3
Each 60 x 40 cm
Courtesy Galerie Hervé Loevenbruck, Paris

Ernesto Caivano (b. 1972, Spain)

**Union and Offerings
(Corpus Callosum, Masculinus, Femininus)**. 2004
Triptych drawing installation
Ink on paper
88,2 x 224,4 cm
21,3 x 224,4 cm
21,3 x 224,4 cm
Courtesy carlier | gebauer, Berlin

Lotte Konow Lund (b. 1967, Norway)

Let it go – The Dürer drawings 1 - 29. 2004-2005
Ink on paper
Each 29,7 x 21 cm
Private Collection, Courtesy Galleri Wang, Oslo

Mindaugas Lukosaitis (b. 1980, Lithuania)

Resistance. 2004
A series of 100 drawings
Pencil on paper
Each 29,7 x 21 cm
Courtesy IBID PROJECTS London & Vilnius

Barry McGee (b. 1966, USA)

Untitled. 2005
24 parts
Pen on paper, found frames
125 x 160 x 10 cm
Courtesy Stuart Shave | Modern Art, London

Julie Mehretu (b. 1970, Ethiopia)

Untitled. 1998
Ink on vellum mounted on board
53.3 x 68.6 cm
Private Collection, Courtesy White Cube, London

Untitled. 1998
Ink on vellum mounted on board
53.3 x 68.6 cm
Private Collection, Courtesy White Cube, London

Untitled. 1999
Ink on vellum mounted on light box
138.4 x 200 cm
Private Collection, Courtesy White Cube, London

Untitled. 2002
Ink on velum and mylar
45.7 x 61 cm
Private Collection, Courtesy White Cube, London

Untitled. 2002
Ink on velum and mylar
45.7 x 61 cm
Private Collection, Courtesy White Cube, London

Untitled. 2002
Ink on velum and mylar
45.7 x 61 cm
Private Collection, Courtesy White Cube, London

Paul Noble (b. 1963, England)

Unified Nobson. 2001
DVD for Projection, 3 minute loop
Courtesy Maureen Paley, London

Sea V, The Carnival Between. 2005
Pencil on paper
Two sections
300 x 200 cm
Courtesy Maureen Paley, London and Gagosian Gallery, New York

Wilhelm Sasnal (b. 1972, Poland)

Untitled. 2003
Ink on paper
41,7 x 29,7 cm
Sadie Coles HQ, London

Untitled. 2004
Ink on paper
29,5 x 42 cm
The Artist, Courtesy Sadie Coles HQ, London

Untitled. 2004
Ink on paper
29,5 x 42 cm
The Artist, Courtesy Sadie Coles HQ, London

Untitled. 2004
Ink on paper
29,5 x 42 cm
The Artist, Courtesy Sadie Coles HQ, London

Untitled. 2004
Ink on paper
29,5 x 42 cm
The Artist, Courtesy Sadie Coles HQ, London

Untitled. 2004
Ink on paper
42 x 59,5 cm
The Artist, Courtesy Sadie Coles HQ, London

Untitled. 2004
Ink on paper
42 x 59,5 cm
The Artist, Courtesy Sadie Coles HQ, London

Untitled. 2004
Ink on paper
59,5 x 42 cm
The Artist, Courtesy Sadie Coles HQ, London

Untitled. 2004
Ink on paper
59,5 x 42 cm
The Artist, Courtesy Sadie Coles HQ, London

Morten Schelde (b. 1972, Denmark)

German Interior. 2004
Pencil on paper
200 x 148 cm
Private Collection

Untitled. 2005
Site-specific installation, wall drawing and framed drawings
Crayon and pencil
Dimensions variable
The Artist, Courtesy Galleri Susanne Ottesen, Copenhagen

Inga Svala Thorsdottir (b. 1966, Iceland)

10 drawings from BORG. 2000
BORG The Hidden Valley (four drawings)
BORG central station
ELDBORG train station
Hallarmuli train station
Bjarnarhafnarfjall train station
Reykjavik train station
Marsh gas factory in BORG

Pen and pencil on paper
Various dimensions
Sammlung Falckenberg, Hamburg

BORG LIGHT 2000. 2000
12 framed drawings of the light in BORG on 12 days and nights
of the year 2000
Pencil and Copic-ink on paper
Each 61,5 x 44 cm
and
12 framed photographs made from scans of documents from
the Icelandic Meteorological Office of Iceland depicted on the
drawings showing the amount of sunshine each day
Each 16 x 44 cm
BORG Collection, Inga Svala Thorsdottir